Jewish Holidays, Jewish Values

Lesson Plan Manual

By Rachael Gelfman Schultz and Aliza Zeff

BEHRMAN HOUSE

Behrman House, Inc.
www.behrmanhouse.com/holidays-values

Design: AURAS Design
Project editor: Dena Neusner
Editorial consultants: Diane Zimmerman, Nathan Weiner
Introduction and chapters 1, 2, 5, 8, 10 by Rachael Gelfman Schultz
Chapters 3, 4, 6, 7, 9 by Aliza Zeff

Springfield, New Jersey 07081
www.behrmanhouse.com

ISBN 978-0-87441-916-0
Printed in the United States of America

Visit www.behrmanhouse.com/holidays-values for more resources.

Contents

Introduction

WHY TEACH JEWISH HOLIDAYS AND JEWISH VALUES TOGETHER?

Jewish Holidays, Jewish Values invites students to explore Jewish holidays through the lens of Jewish values and character development. How can Jewish holidays help us become our best selves—more kind, generous, thoughtful, and happy? How can the Jewish values we learn from these holidays guide us in making decisions in our day-to-day lives? *Jewish Holidays, Jewish Values* will bring energy and depth to our study of Jewish values by showing how they are rooted in the Jewish holidays. By helping students make connections between their Jewish traditions and their everyday lives, students will build and strengthen their Jewish identities.

STRUCTURE OF THE COURSE

Jewish Holidays, Jewish Values follows the course of the Jewish calendar year. Each of the ten chapters focuses on a Jewish holiday or period of holidays, and explores one or two Jewish values through the rituals and themes of that holiday. A brief preface provides a glimpse of the Hebrew calendar, and a concluding page provides a format for students to think about trying new holiday traditions and bringing Jewish values into their lives in new ways. *Jewish Holidays, Jewish Values* consists of two complementary books:

Student Journal

The journal includes creative, interactive activities, integrating Jewish texts with journal writing, art, music, and more. Each chapter begins with a brief introduction to the Jewish holiday and value(s). Activities include hands-on experiences exploring the holiday rituals and the meaning behind them, short Jewish text studies, real-life scenarios and projects where the Jewish values come into play, images to identify and discuss, and word games and puzzles to review and reinforce holiday concepts.

Lesson Plan Manual

This Lesson Plan Manual presents 22 ready-to-use lesson plans of 45 to 50 minutes each for *Jewish Holidays, Jewish Values*. It includes suggestions for teaching every element of the journal. Each chapter begins with an introduction to the Jewish holiday and the Jewish value or values and the connection between them.

USING THIS LESSON PLAN MANUAL

At the start of the year, map out when you plan to teach each chapter. The 22 lessons have been designed so that you can teach an average of one lesson per week. Teaching lessons on the holidays around the time they will be celebrated helps students connect with the learning. This also affords the opportunity to extend the learning through celebration together as a class. Before you begin to teach a holiday, read through the Lesson Plan Manual to familiarize yourself with the chapter. You may choose to use the lessons exactly as they are, or you may adapt the lessons to fit the needs of your class. If you adapt the lessons, it is important to frame your lesson around central questions and goals. This book makes frequent references to images and activities in the journal, and provides the corresponding journal page numbers for your easy reference.

Lesson plans include:

- **Essential Questions:** Overarching questions that reflect the main idea of the lesson
- **Goals:** Specific goals for each lesson that correspond to the concepts and ideas that students should understand when they complete the lesson

- **Introduction:** A brief overview of the lesson, including the Jewish value and its connection to the Jewish holiday
- **Materials Needed:** List of any handouts, art supplies, or other materials necessary for the lesson
- **Activities:** Step-by-step directions for presenting the lesson, including discussion topics, hands-on activities, and individual and group work
- **Enrichment Options:** Optional activities that enrich the students' understanding of the holiday and values
- **Further Resources:** Suggestions for both the teacher's own reference, and for materials and activities for classroom use

TEACHING STRATEGIES AND TIPS

Experiential Learning

Experience plays an important role in the learning process. Take the process of learning to ride a bike, for example. First, we watch others do it, or we listen to someone explain how it is done. Then, we try bike riding ourselves; inevitably, we fall down at first. We reflect on what went wrong and decide how to adjust our approach. That's an effective learning process. We take an action, see the consequences of that action, and then choose to either continue what we've been doing or try a different approach. Our experience of an event and our reflection on that experience allow us to master and internalize what we learned. Now consider the process of learning about the shofar. How different the learning is when we actually see a shofar up close, touch it, listen to its sounds, and blow into it after reading about it.

Jewish holidays are all about living the experience and learning through it. Hearing the piercing sound of the shofar inspires us to reflect on how we can be better people; living in the flimsy sukkah helps us understand how the Israelites lived in the desert; and tasting *maror* teaches us about the bitterness of slavery in Egypt. It is particularly important, therefore, for a course about Jewish holidays to emphasize experiential learning. Each lesson in this manual includes ideas for experiential learning to give students the opportunity to actively experience the lessons presented.

Journal Writing

Personal journal writing helps students reflect on the relevance of Jewish values to their lives. Why is this Jewish value important to me? How can I act on this value in my own life? Each chapter includes open-ended questions for students to respond to by journal writing. Whenever students do journal writing, tell them that their writing is private and for themselves alone. They will not be required to share with other students. At some points in the lessons, students may volunteer to share some of their reflections, but this sharing should not be mandatory.

Project Based Learning

With project based learning, students use the knowledge and skills they have learned in class to solve real-world problems. Individually, or in pairs or groups, students make or do something concrete to demonstrate what they have learned, such as a tzedakah or environmental project. Project based learning is student directed and often collaborative, as students work together to solve a problem. When students learn about Jewish values through project based learning, they gain a deeper understanding of how Jewish values are relevant to their lives. Classes can create their own project based learning experiences based on many of the ideas in *Jewish Holidays, Jewish Values*. For more information on creating exciting project based learning activities in your classroom, read the Project Based Learning section on page 71 of this book or visit www.behrmanhouse.com/project-based-learning.

K-W-L Chart

You may wish to create a K-W-L (Know, Want to Know, Learned) chart about the holidays with your students. You can use a large sheet of chart paper or poster board, and set up the chart like this:

What I Know	What I Want to Know	What I Learned

The K-W-L chart can be used for almost any unit of study. As you study each holiday, begin by asking students what they know about the holiday and recording their responses in the "What I Know" column. You can use this information to clear up misconceptions and determine how much lesson time to spend on the basics of the holiday. Next, ask students what they would like to know about the holiday and what questions they have, and record their suggestions in the middle column. At the end of the unit of study, prompt students to share what they have learned and write their responses in the "What I Learned" column. Check back and make sure their questions from the middle column were addressed. You can keep this chart posted throughout the year or bring it with you and put it on the wall for each class.

Being Inclusive

Children vary in their learning styles. Some students learn best with a hands-on approach, while others do best with a visual or an auditory approach. In general, teachers who present material in many different ways will be able to reach many more children.

Teachers of children with special needs have extra challenges. These children may have a broad range of cognitive, physical, and behavioral disabilities that impact learning. It is always helpful for the education director to find out from parents what accommodations are made for their child in secular school. The suggestions included below are primarily for those children with learning, perceptual, or attention problems.

- For students with attention and auditory processing difficulties, teach in small increments and present one instruction at a time. Ask the children to repeat the instruction to be sure they have processed it.
- For children with attention problems, limit teaching segments to 10 to 15 minutes, and allow for movement between activities.
- For children with attention and visual figure-ground challenges, mask parts of the page so they can see only the section that is being worked on.
- For children with fine motor and handwriting problems, limit the amount of writing, drawing, and cutting that is required. Prepare these difficult parts of a project in advance of the class and have students finish the task. This is an excellent way to engage a classroom *madrich* or *madrichah*. (*The Madrichim Manual* [Behrman House] is an excellent resource for learning how to engage *madrichim* appropriately.)

Remember, the relationships that you build with the students and that they build with one another are as important as the material you teach. Consistently try to model patience and respect for all students.

Interpersonal and Intrapersonal Learners

Some students learn best through interacting with others (interpersonal); some learn best independently (intrapersonal). With this in mind, there are suggestions in the lesson plans for independent work and for activities and discussions with a partner, group, or the whole class. In general, if the lesson plan does not specify that students are meeting with a partner or in a group, plan to have a class discussion.

Group Work

Many of the lessons include suggestions for group work. Whenever possible, plan ahead how you want to form the groups. It is important to change the composition of your groups. For some tasks you will want students with a variety of talents and interests. For others you may choose to group together students with similar skills.

Group work is most successful when every group member knows his or her responsibilities. To help make the group's task clear, prepare written instructions before the class. Many of the lesson plans include such instructions.

Consider creating index cards that describe the jobs of group members. Jobs will vary depending on the type of group work. Some possible jobs include the following:

- Recorder—records the group's suggestions or findings that will be reported to the class
- Reporter—reports the group's work to the class
- Illustrator—draws the group's ideas to be presented to the class
- Investigator—researches to discover information
- Encourager—encourages group members to stay on task
- Reader—reads aloud information to the group

Consider laminating the job description index cards and distributing them each time you do group work.

Integrating Technology

Your students are growing up in a world in which technology is part of their daily lives at home and at school. There are infinite ways that you can take advantage of the Internet and digital applications to deepen understanding, reinforce concepts, share learning with families, and add creativity, interactivity, and excitement to your lessons.

Visit www.behrmanhouse.com/holidays-values. This site provides valuable resources that will enrich and deepen your students' learning about the holidays and values in each chapter, including links to videos, games, puzzles, articles, songs, and more.

For further enrichment, download the free *Jewish Holidays, Jewish Values Game Pack,* filled with fun, content-rich activities and puzzles to play online or print out. Encourage students to explore the Game Pack and play the games at home or in class when time permits.

Note that the Behrman House Online Learning Center offers a platform for sharing information and collaborating on projects. You can find more information about the Online Learning Center here: www.behrmanhouse.com/olc/discover-the-online-learning-center.

The Jewish Year

Before beginning your course of study about the Jewish holidays, introduce your students to the Hebrew calendar.

Ask students for their observations about the dates of the Jewish holidays. If students have noticed that the dates change from year to year, explain that while the dates change every year on the secular (Gregorian) calendar, the holidays are actually on the same date every year on the Hebrew calendar. This is because the two calendars are calculated differently. Encourage students to look up today's date on the Hebrew calendar, as well as any other dates they're interested in (such as birthdays and holidays). Ask students to turn to the journal, page 5, for a brief look at the Hebrew calendar.

If there's time, you can delve further into the Hebrew calendar by exploring these ideas:

Ask students why they think each day on the Hebrew calendar begins in the evening, not in the morning. Explain that on the very first day of the Creation of the world, the Torah tells us, "There was evening and there was morning, a first day." (Genesis 1:5)

The first day of each Hebrew month is called Rosh Chodesh, which means "head of the month" in Hebrew. Provide each student with a calendar page with the Hebrew dates filled in for all the days in the month. Then ask them to look at the moon each night for one month and sketch the shape of the moon in the corresponding box on their calendar. Since the Hebrew calendar is based on the cycles of the moon, the first sliver of the new moon will appear on the first day of the Hebrew month, and there will always be a full moon on the fifteenth day of the month.

Chapter

1

THE HIGH HOLIDAYS

Returning to Our Best Selves • *Teshuvah*

Rosh Hashanah and Yom Kippur, and the days between them, are a time to focus on *teshuvah* (repentance or return), on striving to be the best we can be. The High Holidays are the perfect time to begin our study of Jewish holidays and Jewish values, because they are all about new beginnings and changing the way we act. This entire book is built around the premise that we have the power to change and develop our character.

The first lesson in this chapter focuses on Rosh Hashanah as a celebration of new beginnings, when we think about what we can do in the New Year to strive to become our best selves. The second lesson focuses on Yom Kippur and doing *teshuvah*. These lessons are an opportunity to think big about what we like about our character and what we wish was different, and to begin to create an action plan to make change in our lives.

Lesson 1: Rosh Hashanah and New Beginnings

Essential Questions: How can the rituals and traditions of Rosh Hashanah help us to make new beginnings in the way we act and relate to one another? What will we do differently in the New Year?

Goals: Students will:

1. Experience Rosh Hashanah rituals and traditions.
2. Explore how these rituals and traditions help us to make new beginnings.
3. Discuss the mitzvah of forgiveness and how they can fulfill this mitzvah in their lives.

Introduction

On Rosh Hashanah, the Jewish New Year, we celebrate new beginnings. We ask forgiveness of God and each other for the mistakes we have made over the course of the past year. We pray that next year, we will be more kind, generous, and sensitive. In this lesson, students express their personal prayers for the coming year, while experiencing some of the central Rosh Hashanah rituals and exploring what it means to ask (and offer) forgiveness.

Materials Needed

- A shofar, or several shofars, if possible
- Small paper plates, bowls, and napkins
- Traditional foods such as apples and honey, and pomegranates
- Optional: a variety of small foods such as dried fruits, nuts, and candies (Make sure to check first with the education director about guidelines for food shared in school, such as keeping kosher and allergies.)
- Blank pieces of paper, cut into strips

Advance Preparation

A week before this class, explain to students that they should bring in a food representing their wish for the next year (see Activity 2, Rosh Hashanah Seder, below for a more detailed explanation). Send a follow-up email to parents. (Check first about food guidelines, as noted above.)

Activities

1. Getting Started: "Wake Up"—The Sound of the Shofar (5 minutes)

If possible, bring the students to the sanctuary and ask someone to blow the shofar for them. Alternatively, ask someone to blow the shofar in the classroom. While students listen to the shofar, ask them to sit quietly and think about something good that they did during the past year. Then, as the shofar is blown again, ask students to think about something they did for which they would like to ask forgiveness. Lastly, while a third note of the shofar is blown, ask students to think about a personal prayer for the New Year.

If time allows, bring in alcohol wipes and several shofars, and give each student an opportunity to blow the shofar while thinking about his or her personal prayers. (If you are unable to have someone blow a shofar, you can play an audio recording or show a video of a shofar being blown.)

Ask each student to write his or her own personal prayer for the New Year on page 6 of the journal.

2. Rosh Hashanah Seder (20 minutes)

Advance preparation: A week before today's class, explain to students that you will be making a Rosh Hashanah seder as a class. Many Jewish families of Middle Eastern descent have the custom of making a seder on the first evening of Rosh Hashanah, where they gather together to eat symbolic foods just as we do at the Passover seder. (This custom is less common in the United States, where many families come from Eastern Europe.) Each food at the Rosh Hashanah seder symbolizes a prayer for the coming year. Apples and honey (or challah dipped in honey) are one example; they represent our wish for a sweet new year. Another example is the pomegranate, which represents our wish that our *mitzvot* be as numerous as its seeds.

Ask each student to think of a food that represents his or her wishes for the coming year, and to bring enough of the food to give each student in the class a small taste (for example, one slice of an apple for each student, or one chocolate chip). Be sure to check first with the education director about synagogue rules regarding keeping kosher and allergies. If students are not allowed to bring food to your synagogue, let students suggest the foods that the school can then supply.

On the day of the seder, go around the room and ask each student to share his or her food and wish for the New Year with the class. Bring in traditional foods as well, such as apples and honey, and pomegranates, to enrich your class seder. You may also bring in some small foods, such as dried fruit, nuts, and candies, so that students who forget to bring in food can choose from the options available. Encourage students to listen carefully to their classmates' wishes, and decide which ones they'd like to include in their journal, page 7, along with their own wishes.

3. Tashlich (10 minutes)

Ask students to write down their mistakes privately on small slips of paper. Examples could include, "I pulled my little sister's hair," or "I said something mean about my friend behind her back." Then do a symbolic *tashlich* ceremony with the class, where each student rips up these slips of paper and throws them out. As they throw out the paper, students can recite the verse in their journal (page 8) from Micah 7:19, which is traditionally recited at *tashlich.*

If there is time, take the students outside to a body of water and do *tashlich* there, by throwing the slips of paper into the water. Or bring in a child's pool or bucket to the classroom.

Ask students: How would it feel if your mistakes were really washed away? How does doing *tashlich* make you feel?

4. What Would You Do? (10 minutes)

Ask students to read the dilemma on page 9 of the journal by themselves or act out the confrontation in pairs, and then write down what they would do to resolve it. When they're done writing, students can debate the issue. Make sure that different students represent the different sides of the argument, stating why they would or would not ask for forgiveness.

Explain that during the High Holiday season, it is not enough to ask forgiveness from God; it is a mitzvah to ask forgiveness from each other. Ask students: Why do you think there is a mitzvah to ask forgiveness and to forgive? Why is it difficult to do this mitzvah?

5. Wrapping It Up: Asking Forgiveness (5 minutes)

Ask students to privately fill in the blanks in the journal, page 10. Then encourage students to actually go and ask forgiveness, now or when they get home—don't just talk about it! Ask students to think about how they feel both before and after they ask forgiveness, and how it feels to forgive someone.

Enrichment Options

Rosh Hashanah Cards: Some people write Rosh Hashanah greeting cards to family and friends, wishing them a good and sweet New Year, *Shanah tovah u'metukah*. Give students paper and markers/crayons to make their own Rosh Hashanah cards for themselves and others. On the cards for themselves, students write about the new things they would like to do in the coming year, such as take an art class or cook dinner once a week. In the cards for others, they write about new things they would like to do together with that person.

Further Resources

Visit www.behrmanhouse.com/holidays-values for more Rosh Hashanah seder ideas and examples of traditional foods.

Lesson 2: Yom Kippur and *Teshuvah*

Essential Questions: How can the High Holiday season help us to do *teshuvah* in our lives? How can doing *teshuvah* help me become my best self?

Goals: Students will:

1. Define the value of *teshuvah* (repentance or return).
2. Understand how the rituals and traditions of Yom Kippur help us focus on doing *teshuvah.*
3. Reflect on how they can do *teshuvah* in their lives.

Introduction

Yom Kippur is the culmination of the *teshuvah* season. *Teshuvah* literally means to "return" and is often translated as "repentance." *Teshuvah* describes our efforts to return to our best selves, to fulfill our potential. When we do *teshuvah,* we look at our lives and think about how we can become better people, and then we act on it. In this lesson, we explore what the rituals and traditions of Yom Kippur teach us about *teshuvah.* Then we make a plan for how we as a class can help each other do *teshuvah.*

Materials Needed

- Poster board and markers

Activities

1. Getting Started: Jonah in the Fish's Belly, and Teshuvah (15 minutes)

Read the summary of the Jonah story together on page 11, or, if there's time, read the first two chapters of the book of Jonah. Discuss: What do you think inspired Jonah to do *teshuvah*? What else can inspire a person to do *teshuvah*?

Ask students to read Making Meaning, on page 11, and then draw a picture of what inspires them to do *teshuvah,* using the space inside the fish's belly.

2. Fasting (10 minutes)

One of the central prohibitions on Yom Kippur is eating. Discuss: Why do you think Jews fast on Yom Kippur? (*Fasting helps us focus on prayer and teshuvah without the distractions of eating.)* Ask students to respond to the prompts in their student books, page 12. Then ask them to turn to the person next to them and share what they chose to give up on Yom Kippur and why.

3. Kol Nidrei (5 minutes)

Read the section about Kol Nidrei together on page 13, and ask each student to answer the questions privately. The Torah emphasizes the importance of keeping our word, so Kol Nidrei is a way of cancelling promises to God that we are unable to keep. Kol Nidrei frees us to be ambitious in our new resolutions to God, while letting us be at peace with our past failures.

4. Try This: Teshuvah Contract (15 minutes)

Explain that the class is going to make a *teshuvah* contract, a list of specific things students will work on doing better this year. This list should include things we can do better within the classroom environment. For example, we will do our best to listen to the teacher and each other, to speak kindly to each other, to help each other, and to give tzedakah each week using a class tzedakah box.

Create a poster that you can hang in the classroom entitled "Our Class *Teshuvah* Contract" and list the different items. Invite students to decorate the poster and hang it up in a prominent place in the classroom, where it can remind students of their contract throughout the year.

5. Wrapping It Up (5 minutes)

Discuss: How can we help ourselves and our fellow students to follow this *teshuvah* contract? Often, people make a lot of resolutions on Rosh Hashanah and Yom Kippur, but they have trouble following through after the High Holiday season is over. Think about how you can remind each other of the contract, such as using some sort of hand signal to show your appreciation when someone does something in the contract, or pointing at the poster quietly when someone isn't following the contract.

Chapter

2

SUKKOT

Humility • *Anavah,* and Gratitude • *Hakarot Hatov*

Sukkot, like many biblical holidays, has a historical aspect and an agricultural aspect. The Torah teaches us to spend time in *sukkot*, temporary huts, during this holiday to remember the *sukkot* our ancestors lived in when they were wandering in the desert. The holiday of Sukkot also celebrates the completion of the harvest, when Jews give thanks to God for the blessings of the land.

In this chapter, we will discuss two connected values that we can learn from these two aspects of Sukkot—humility (*anavah*) and gratitude (*hakarat hatov*). Lesson 3 will focus on the sukkah and the humility this mitzvah teaches us. Lesson 4 will focus on the completion of the harvest and giving thanks for the blessings in our lives.

Lesson 3: The Sukkah: Living with Humility

Essential Questions: What can we learn from our Sukkot celebrations about the value of humility, and how can this value guide us in our lives?

Goals: Students will:

1. Explain the mitzvah of the sukkah and the reasoning behind it.
2. Define *anavah* (humility) and provide concrete examples of this value.
3. Reflect on how understanding the value of humility can help them make better decisions in their lives.

Introduction

On the holiday of Sukkot, the Torah commands Jews to leave their comfortable houses and their many possessions to live in a sukkah—a simple, flimsy structure—for a week. Even though today many of us do not actually live in the sukkah, we can still eat meals or spend time in a sukkah either at our local synagogue or in a family's backyard. The sukkah reminds us of how our ancestors lived while wandering in the desert. In this lesson, we will explore how the mitzvah of spending time in the sukkah can teach us to lead more modest, humble lives—lives of *anavah.*

Materials Needed

- (Optional) Building materials for a model sukkah, such as small sticks and branches, modeling clay, cardboard boxes, foil, pipe cleaners, and construction paper

Activities

1. Getting Started: "You Shall Live in Sukkot" (10 minutes)

Ask one student to read the verse from Leviticus, on page 14 of the journal, out loud.

As a class, discuss:

- What do you think it would feel like to really live in a sukkah for a week? What would you enjoy? What would you miss about your home?
- How would living in a sukkah for a week make you feel about your home and your belongings? *(It would make me appreciate what I have; it would make me realize that maybe I do not need everything that I thought I needed.)*
- Why is it important to remember that our ancestors lived in *sukkot* when they were wandering in the desert? *(Remembering that our people used to live in these simple huts prevents us from becoming arrogant about our comfortable homes full of stuff and helps us appreciate what we have.)*
- How could remembering that our ancestors lived in *sukkot* change the way we look at those who have less than we do? *(It reminds us not to look down on those people who have fewer things than we do because our ancestors also once lived much more simply.)*

Give students a few minutes to journal their responses to the prompts on page 14.

2. My Sukkah (15 minutes)

Explain that spending time in the sukkah encourages us to ask the question: What is really important to us? What things do we own that we really need or that really make our lives better, and what things do we own that are unnecessary or distract us from what is really important to us?

Each student designs his or her own model sukkah in the journal, page 15. Remind students to include only the bare minimum, to focus on the idea of what is really necessary and important.

Optional: If you choose, give students materials so they can each build their own model sukkah. When students have completed their *sukkot*, you may display the *sukkot* in the classroom. Students may walk around and look at other *sukkot*. In pairs, students can share what they made and explain what they chose to put in the sukkah and why.

3. Making Meaning: Anavah (5 minutes)

Ask a student to read the word *anavah* and its definition on page 16 of the journal. Discuss with the class what it means to be humble, and ask them to give concrete examples. *(not to brag, not to show off, not to buy things or clothes that we don't need just so that other people will think we are cool, to have a realistic understanding of our own strengths and weaknesses)*

Ask students to fill in the prompts in the journal privately.

4. What Would You Do? (10 minutes)

Invite a few students to the front of the room to act out the scenario described on page 16 of the journal, imagining the conversation about test scores. What do you say about your high grade? Or do you not say anything at all? How do your friends react to what you say? Remind students to pay attention not only to what they say but also to their facial expressions and body language.

Discuss:

- How did your words or actions make your friends feel?
- Is it okay to say that you are proud of what you accomplished? Why or why not?
- If it is okay to talk about it, how do you tell your friends about your grade? Do you say, "I am so smart, I got a 100," "I worked so hard to get a 100," or "My big brother helped me study a lot, and its partly thanks to him that I got a 100"? What is the difference between these ways of talking about your grade?

5. Wrapping It Up (10 minutes)

In small groups, ask students to brainstorm and act out other situations or dilemmas in which they can demonstrate *anavah*.

Lesson 4: The Jewish Thanksgiving

Essential Questions: What are we grateful for? How does expressing gratitude help us to be better people?

Goals: Students will:

1. Understand the mitzvah of the *lulav* and *etrog* and discuss the tradition behind it.
2. Define *hakarat hatov*, "gratitude," and give concrete examples.
3. Reflect on how they can show more *hakarat hatov* in their own lives.

Introduction

On Sukkot, biblical Jews celebrated the completion of the harvest by giving thanks to God. They took the *lulav* and *etrog* and rejoiced before God. Today, although most of us are no longer farmers, we continue to take the opportunity to give thanks on Sukkot. This lesson explores how celebrating Sukkot reminds us to appreciate the blessings in our lives and to show more *hakarat hatov*, "gratitude."

Materials Needed

- *Lulav* and *etrog,* if available (if not, you can create a model *lulav* and *etrog* using construction paper or poster board)
- Colored pencils or markers

Activities

1. Getting Started: Personality Quiz (10 minutes)

Ask students to quietly take the personality quiz on page 17 in the journal. Urge them to be as realistic as possible—not to write down what they wish they would do, but what they would most likely do in that situation.

After the students have completed the quiz, ask them to read the results to themselves.

Discuss with the class: What are the pros and cons of each of the three kinds of responses? Emphasize to the students that pride, humility, and gratitude each have their place—the question is how and where.

2. The Jewish Thanksgiving (20 minutes)

Ask one student to read aloud the verses from Leviticus 23:39-40 in the journal, page 18.

Ask students to complete the activity, comparing Thanksgiving and Sukkot. Emphasize that both of these holidays were originally festivals celebrating the completion of the harvest, when people gathered together to thank God for their blessings.

Discuss:

- Why do you think the Torah tells the ancient Israelites to "rejoice before Adonai your God," rather than just celebrating on their own? *(They were acknowledging that their achievements were not only due to their own talents and hard work, but to the gifts given to them by God, such as fertile land and rain.)*
- When you celebrate your own successes and milestones, how (if at all) is your celebration a way of saying thank you to God or to the people who helped make it possible? Think about how you celebrate getting an award in school or at an extracurricular activity, or how your family and community celebrates milestones like births, bar and bat mitzvahs, or weddings.

Explain that the *lulav* and *etrog* are otherwise known as the four species, and they include: 1) the *lulav* or palm branch, 2) the myrtle branch, 3) the willow branch (the three branches are held together), and 4) the *etrog*, a citrus fruit. Biblical Jews used the four species on Sukkot to give thanks to God for the completed harvest. The four species represent the fruits of the land that they had just finished harvesting.

If possible, bring in a *lulav* and *etrog* to show students, identifying each of the species. If you don't have a real *lulav* and *etrog*, go online and show students photographs.

Recite the blessing together and show students how to shake the *lulav* and *etrog* (journal, page 18). Ask students to think of a time they worked hard at something and were successful. Then let them, one at a time, shake the *lulav* and *etrog* while they express their gratitude to God (out loud or privately) for that success.

Visit www.behrmanhouse.com/holidays-values for a video on how to shake the *lulav* and *etrog* and the blessing.

3. Making Meaning: Hakarat Hatov (5 minutes)

Ask a student to read the phrase *hakarat hatov* in Hebrew and its definition. Discuss the students' responses to the questions on page 19 of the journal. (*If we are humble, we don't just congratulate ourselves for our accomplishments; we also thank those who made it possible. We recognize that we could not have done it alone.)*

4. Ushpizin: Inviting Guests (10 minutes)

Ask students: Who would you like to invite into your sukkah? Think of one person in Jewish history whom you would like to meet, and imagine your conversation with him or her. Write down the conversation on page 19 of the journal, and then act it out in pairs.

5. Wrapping It Up: My Hallel (5 minutes)

Explain to students that another way that Jews celebrate Sukkot today is by saying Hallel, a collection of psalms to thank God for all the good that God does for us. Read Psalms 118:21, "I give thanks to You, for You have answered me." Then ask students to write their own Hallel prayers on page 20, to give thanks for the blessings in their lives. Encourage students to be as specific as possible. Students may also illustrate their Hallel prayers using colored pencils or markers. Invite volunteers to share their illustrated prayers, and collect them into a class Hallel book. Send a copy home with each child.

Enrichment Options

Gratitude Begins at Home: Ask students to choose a time to sit down with their family and show some *hakarat hatov.* A good time for this could be at a family meal, in a sukkah if possible. Each person in the family takes turns going around and saying thank you to every other member of the family for something specific that person did. When students return to class, ask them:

- How did it feel to thank your family members?
- How did it feel to be thanked?

Decorating Your Sukkah: Students create their own sukkah decorations representing the blessings in their lives for which they are grateful. Encourage them to focus on things they might sometimes take for granted (family and friends, health, a warm home, nature), rather than just material possessions. They can use construction paper, scissors, markers, paint, etc. Also consider using recycled materials, such as water bottles, empty cereal boxes, and paper towel tubes. Get permission to hang the decorations in your synagogue's sukkah.

Further Resources

Visit www.behrmanhouse.com/holidays-values for guidelines for building a sukkah and more insights about why we sit in the sukkah.

Chapter 3

SIMCHAT TORAH

Rejoicing • *Simchah*

On Simchat Torah, we celebrate the completion of a full cycle of reading the weekly Torah portions, and we begin a new cycle of reading the Torah from the beginning. Simchat Torah means "joy in the Torah" in Hebrew. In order to show our joy in the Torah, the source of our traditions, laws, values, and stories, it is traditional to dance and sing with the Torah. On Simchat Torah we are, in fact, commanded to rejoice with the Torah and with our community. It is through our celebrations that we demonstrate and renew our commitment to learning the Torah.

In this chapter, we will explore the value of *simchah*, "happiness" and "rejoicing," and how we can embrace this value in an appropriate way. We will focus on the idea of expressing joy as a way of affirming our values on Simchat Torah or anytime, and we will reflect on different ways in which we express joy or *simchah*. In lesson 5, we will investigate how we celebrate the Torah through our holiday traditions and how the Torah scroll and its ornaments demonstrate our devotion to *simchah*. In lesson 6, we will explore the value of *simchah* more deeply, by examining how we express it in our daily lives.

Lesson 5: Rejoicing with the Torah

Essential Questions: How does the Torah guide us in living a life of joy? How is Simchat Torah a model for the Jewish value of rejoicing?

Goals: Students will:

1. Recognize that the reading of Torah is cyclical and that when we finish reading it, we celebrate as a community.
2. Understand the physical parts of the Torah scroll and its ornaments.
3. Explain how happiness and joy are central to Simchat Torah traditions.

Introduction

After a sequence of holidays that require introspection, asking for forgiveness, and a lot of physical and spiritual preparation, Simchat Torah provides a much-needed celebration. On this holiday, we thank God for the Torah, and we rejoice in the accomplishment of having completed the yearly cycle of Torah readings. Even if your community reads on a triennial system (one third of each Torah portion is read every week, taking three years to read it in full), on Simchat Torah, you begin anew with Genesis.

On Simchat Torah, we are commanded to rejoice with the Torah. For this lesson, students will learn about the parts of a Torah scroll, and will connect the traditions of Simchat Torah to the central notion of *simchah*, "joy," which defines the nature of the holiday.

Materials Needed

- Markers or colored pencils
- Access to a Torah scroll

Advance Preparation

Ask the education director or rabbi's permission to take a close look at the Torah scrolls in the sanctuary. Enlist some adult helpers. (See Activity 5, below.)

Activities

1. Getting Started: What Makes You Want to Celebrate? (5 minutes)

Ask students to answer the questions on page 21 of the journal.

2. Making Meaning: Simchah (5 minutes)

Ask a student to read the word *simchah* and its meaning on page 22 of the journal. Ask: What are some of the ways you show *simchah*?

3. What Does Simchat Torah Mean? (5 minutes)

Ask your class to look carefully at the name of the holiday, and discuss the meaning of the two words. Explain that the word *simchat* is related to *simchah.*

Ask students to design an app button or book cover on page 22, based on the two words that make up the name of this holiday. Allow time for students to share their drawings with the class or with a partner.

Discuss:

- In what different ways is *simchah* shown in your design?
- Which concept was central in your design, *simchah* or Torah? Why?
- How does your design show the importance of Torah in your life?

4. How Do We Celebrate? (15 minutes)

Explain to your students that there is a lot of celebration going on during Simchat Torah. Ask students what traditions they know of that are practiced on Simchat Torah. (*reading the end and then the beginning of the Torah; honoring a special member of the community with the first* aliyah*; waving flags; singing and dancing in* hakafot *[singular,* hakafah*], the seven rounds of singing and dancing we do in the synagogue on Simchat Torah; unrolling an entire Torah scroll around the sanctuary*)

Divide students into small groups, and ask each group to choose one of the three activities—dancing, singing, or reading—from the journal, page 23. Give students 5 minutes to prepare, and then let groups take turns leading the class in their interpretation of the activity. Alternatively, you may want to lead one or more of these activities with the whole class.

If your class would like to act out a *hakafah* with a real Torah scroll, make sure you have permission from the rabbi or education director—and at least one other adult present—to remove a Torah from the Ark. Your model *hakafah* will include singing, marching around the room or sanctuary, and dancing around the Torah. If you don't have access to an actual Torah, you can act it out with props.

Visit www.behrmanhouse.com/holidays-values to learn how to dance a horah, and to hear the song "Sisu V'simchu."

5. Investigating the Torah (20 minutes)

Get the rabbi or education director's permission to look at the Torah scrolls, and, with the help of some other adults, to remove a Torah scroll from the Ark.

Bring the class to the sanctuary, or bring a Torah scroll to the classroom. Set up two rows of chairs facing one another and ask students to sit so that their knees are nearly touching the person across from them. Begin by placing the Torah upright in one student's lap at the head of the rows.

Help the students pass the Torah carefully down the row. As each student holds the Torah, ask him or her to identify what they see. Be sure students notice these items: the *keter* (crown) or *rimmonim* (decorative items placed on top of the ends of the rollers), breastplate (decorative metal plate), mantle (cloth cover), and *yad* (pointer, used by the Torah reader to keep his or her place while reading).

Help students carefully remove these items as they are identified. Then identify and remove the binder or belt (cloth band that holds the Torah closed), and point out the *atzei chayim* (wooden rollers).

Once you have the accessories off the Torah, carefully unroll the scroll on a table or the reader's desk, with the assistance of another adult. Invite students to come close and get a good look, but remind them not to touch the parchment. Ask students what they see. Help them notice these things: parchment (made from the skin of a kosher animal), breaks between *parashot* (portions), some letters that are bigger than others, and stitching between sections of parchment. Challenge students to look for any words or letters that they can read or recognize in the text.

Ask students to respond to the prompts on page 24 of their journals. Then discuss:

- Why do we have so many ritual items for dressing the Torah? Why do we handle the Torah so carefully, taking care not to damage it in any way? *(to emphasize the importance of the Torah, to protect the holiness of the scroll)*
- Explain to students that a scribe who writes a Torah scroll is called a *sofer*, and there are many laws for writing a Torah scroll. For example, there are specific laws regarding how each letter is constructed. Other laws specify that only black ink is allowed, the parchment must be made from the skin of a kosher animal, the scribe cannot write the text from memory, each sheet of parchment must be checked by other Torah experts, and more. Ask students why they think there are so many rules for writing a Torah scroll. *(again, to emphasize the importance of the Torah, to protect the holiness of the scroll)*
- Why is the Torah so important? (*It is the source of stories, traditions, values, and laws of our people; it brings us together as a community; it teaches us how to be our best selves and how to improve the world; it is the basis of our Jewish identity.*)

Finish by carefully rolling the Torah up and dressing it, having students take the lead putting the accessories back on in the correct order.

Enrichment Options

Model Edible Torah Scrolls: Using pretzel sticks, fruit leather and a variety of candies, frosting, and/or sprinkles for the breastplate and crown, have students identify each part of the Torah as they make an edible model. Have students take digital photos of their creation and label each part.

Design Your Own Simchat Torah Flag: Recently, the Masorti (Conservative) Movement in Israel designed a new flag for Simchat Torah. Visit www.behrmanhouse.com/holidays-values for a link to print a picture of the flag. Have students look at that flag, as well as others used in past decades, and then design their own, according to how they envision the celebration.

Further Resources

For further resources visit www.behrmanhouse.com/holidays-values for links to more information on Simchat Torah traditions as well as games, puzzles, crafts and more.

Lesson 6: *Simchah* in Our Lives

Essential Questions: Why and when does Judaism emphasize the value of *simchah*? What role does the Torah play in our happiness?

Goals: Students will:

1. Differentiate between personal and communal happiness.
2. Identify appropriate ways in which we express *simchah*, happiness.
3. Explain how expressing joy helps us affirm our values on Simchat Torah or anytime.

Introduction

On Simchat Torah, we are commanded to rejoice with the Torah. As humans, we express our happiness in different ways, and our celebrations are an expression of what is important to us. In this lesson, students will create an artistic or visual representation of the value of happiness in their lives.

Materials Needed

- Post-it Notes or index cards

Activities

1. Getting Started: What Would You Do? (10 minutes)

Ask students to read and respond to the situation in the journal, page 25.

Follow up as a class by asking volunteers to share their answers. Ask students the following questions: What kinds of emotions would you feel in this situation? *(disappointment, jealousy, happiness, confusion)* What might the other person feel? *(happiness, empathy, confusion, excitement)*

Explain that all of these emotions are natural and that when we feel disappointed in our own achievements, it can be hard to express happiness for someone else's. But by sharing our friend's *simchah*, we demonstrate that we care for her and that we value loyalty, hard work, and friendship.

2. Simchah in Our Lives (10 minutes)

Remind students that on Simchat Torah, we are commanded to rejoice. But what does that mean? What is *simchah,* and how do we express and share it? Split the students into *chevruta* pairs and ask them to read the text about joy on page 26 of their journal, and the Did You Know sidebar, and then discuss or write their responses to the prompts.

Ask what values are demonstrated by thousands of people celebrating Simchat Torah in the streets of New York City? *(joy in the Torah, pride in being Jewish)*

3. What Makes You Happy? (20 minutes)

Ask students to sit in a circle, then hand each student a Post-it Note or index card. Ask them to write down one thing that makes them happy. Remember, it cannot be a material object. Encourage students to really think for a moment of something that brings them the type of joy they discussed with their *chevruta*, in the previous activity. *(Some examples may be listening to music, being with friends, helping someone in need, getting ready for Shabbat, doing something creative, or walking the dog.)*

Once they have each written something, have them pass their notes around the circle. As they receive each note, they should read it and decide whether or not this brings them happiness as well. If so, they put a check mark on it. If not, they simply pass it on. Students should continue passing the notes until they get their own card back.

Discuss as a class:

- What does it mean if you have a lot of check marks on your Post-it Note? *(Others feel happiness from this too; others value this, just as you do.)*
- What does it mean if you don't have a lot of check marks? *(You have found something unique that makes you happy.)* How can others share this with you, even if it's not their natural choice?

Ask for volunteers to share what they wrote and what their choice says about what they value in their lives. *(They like animals, they feel good when they help others, their family is important to them, etc.)*

4. Wrapping It Up: Plan a Torah Party (10 minutes)

Expressing joy is a way of affirming our values. When we're happy about something, we usually want to share that happiness with someone. Explain this idea to your students, and remind them that during this time of year, as we've been studying, we are especially happy for the gift of the Torah.

Ask students to brainstorm appropriate ways to celebrate, to show our joy in the Torah. (*sing, dance, eat good food, create and share artwork or a skit*) Suggest that the class might want to plan a Torah party, to share their joy in the Torah with another class or with their friends and family members. Put students into groups and assign each group one aspect of the party planning, which they can work on outside of class. (*music, decorations, activity, food, time and place*)

Enrichment Options

Small Symbols: The mezuzah reminds us of our joy in being Jewish. It has a scroll inside with text that comes directly from the Torah. Bring in a mezuzah or see if you can borrow one from the gift shop. Open it and show the scroll to the students. Discuss similarities and differences to the Torah. How does the mezuzah remind us of our connection to God and the joy we feel each day or on holidays like Simchat Torah?

Further Resources

For further resources visit www.behrmanhouse.com/holidays-values for links to more resources about Simchat Torah, including a video showing a scribe writing a mezuzah.

Chapter 4

SHABBAT

Holy Time and Space • *Bein Kodesh L'chol,* and Peace • *Shalom*

Shabbat, the seventh day of the week, is a day of rest. Our Shabbat blessings and traditions help us set the tone for a day of peace and wholeness.

An important element of Shabbat is the concept of holy time and space. In this chapter, we will explore the transition between "holy" time and regular or everyday time. In Hebrew, this transition is called *bein kodesh l'chol.* Why is it important to mark transitions in our lives, both the significant and insignificant, and how do we do this? Shabbat is bookended with traditions that help us physically and spiritually mark the day. We will investigate ways in which we acknowledge that Shabbat is different from the rest of the week. We can "unplug" or spend more time with family, and doing so helps to mark this transition.

In lesson 7, we will look closely at the main traditions and blessings of Shabbat that help make it a day of rest. In lesson 8, we will explore the idea of making transitions, and investigate ways in which our traditions can help differentiate *bein kodesh l'chol,* between holy time (Shabbat) and regular time (the rest of the week). In lesson 9, we will examine the concept of peace and ways in which we can bring peacefulness into our homes on Shabbat.

Lesson 7: Day of Rest

Essential Question: How does observing Shabbat as a day of rest bring holiness into our lives?

Goals: Students will:

1. Identify the main traditions of Shabbat, including candle lighting, Kiddush, Hamotzi, going to synagogue, and hearing the Torah reading.
2. Recognize the variety of family traditions that make Shabbat special and help to sanctify it as a day of rest.

Introduction

The idea of observing Shabbat comes from the Torah. In the book of Genesis, Creation takes six days. Then "God blessed the seventh day and declared it holy, because on it God rested from all the work of creation that God had done." (Genesis 2:3)

Throughout history, Jews have tried to follow God's example by resting on Shabbat. This day of rest includes a variety of important practices that help to make the day holy, including lighting candles, saying Kiddush, blessing and eating challah, going to synagogue, and hearing the Torah portion or *parashah*. In this lesson, we will consider where these traditions come from and what they mean, intertwining the idea of rest throughout.

Materials Needed

- Challah
- Grape Juice
- Shabbat candlesticks, candles, and matches (Get permission from the education director before lighting them.)

Advance Preparation

The week before this lesson, send students home with a note asking them to bring to class any Shabbat items that they use in their homes, from candlesticks to challah plates, Kiddush cups to Havdalah sets. Remind students that they must have permission to bring in their item. As an alternative, students could bring in a photo of the object.

Activities

1. Getting Started: Our Day of Rest (5 minutes)

Ask students to write an acrostic poem about Shabbat on page 28 of their journal. Each line should start with a letter of the word *peace*.

Ask your students: What does Shabbat mean to you? What kind of atmosphere could Shabbat rest bring to you or your home?

2. And on the Seventh Day... (5 minutes)

Explain that the word *Shabbat* comes from a Hebrew root meaning "rest from work." Ask students to look at the photos on page 29 of the journal, representing the six days of Creation. The Torah says that God blessed the seventh day and then rested. Ask students to draw a picture representing Shabbat in the empty box. Allow them to share their drawings or thoughts with the class.

3. Welcoming Shabbat (25 minutes)

Ask a volunteer to read aloud the midrash (story) on page 30 of the journal, about how Abraham's wife Sarah lit Shabbat candles.

Explain that because candle lighting is a tradition and not a Jewish law, there are lots of ways to do it. Some people light one candle for each person in the family. Some cover their heads; others sing wordless melodies before the blessing. Ask your students if their families have any unique traditions.

Ask students to show the class any Shabbat items that they brought in. Explain to students that part of what creates holy time, on Shabbat, is that we take the time to use our special family Kiddush cups, candlesticks, and other objects, and to share stories at a Shabbat meal. Allow volunteers to share any family stories about the objects they brought in.

Set out Shabbat candles and light them (or pretend to light them). Practice the blessing together, on page 30 of the journal. Prompt students to sit quietly and watch the flames for a minute to get a sense of peacefulness. Then ask students: What atmosphere is created when candles are lit? What does candlelight make you think of? What are you grateful for on Shabbat? Invite students to decorate the candles in their journals with words or phrases that come to mind, then discuss as a class. Have them imagine not only warmth and light, but also rest and peacefulness. You might guide them toward the following thoughts:

- *Candles bring more light into a world filled with darkness.*
- *Light casts a warm, peaceful, comforting glow on the Shabbat table and the home.*
- *We are grateful for light and warmth and peace, and for all that we have (during World War II, candles were hard to get, so many people couldn't light them).*
- *The flame represents how the Jewish people have survived through so many difficult times in our history, and though our flame might flicker, it doesn't go out.*

Share the grape juice and challah with students, and practice saying the blessings, which are in the journal, page 31. If time permits, introduce students to the full Kiddush, which can be found online, and discuss the meaning of the text.

4. Going to Synagogue (10 minutes)

If possible, bring your students to the sanctuary for this section of the lesson. (Note: if you've lit candles in the previous activity, explain that we normally don't blow out Shabbat candles, but in the interest of safety, we will put the flames out before leaving the room.)

One important way to acknowledge Shabbat is by spending time with our community. Ask: Why do people go to synagogue? *(to participate in worship services, hear the weekly parashah—Torah portion, and spend meaningful time with family or friends)* Ask: Why is it important to be with a community? *(to build relationships, support each other, have a place where we belong)*

Ask the class to mix and match the sentence parts on page 32 of the journal, identifying important areas of the sanctuary. They can draw lines to put the sentence parts in order.

Answers: Here is the chart rearranged with the sentence parts in the correct order.

Start here: (1)	**(2)**	**(3)**	**(4)**	**(5)**
The ***bimah*** is…	the raised platform…	where the Torah reading takes place…	and it's raised above the ground…	so that the whole congregation can see.
The **reader's desk** (or lectern) is…	the table on the *bimah*…	on which the Torah is placed when it is read…	and it's in the front or center of the room…	so that the whole congregation can see.
The ***Aron Hakodesh*** is…	the Ark, or cabinet,…	in which the Torah scrolls are kept…	and it's usually located on the eastern wall…	to face the holy city of Jerusalem.
The ***Ner Tamid*** is…	the eternal lamp…	that hangs over the Ark…	and it's always lit…	to represent God's eternal presence.

Explain that each week, we read a portion of the Torah, called the *parashah.*

5. Wrapping It Up: Did You Know? (5 minutes)

People of other religions and cultures often celebrate a day of rest, too. Ask for a volunteer to read the examples on page 33 of the journal. Ask students which Jewish traditions are most meaningful to them as a way to acknowledge our day of rest. *(Answers may include: saying blessings, sharing family stories, using sacred objects, spending time with our community at the synagogue, hearing the parashah.)* In what other ways do students make Shabbat special, different, or holy as a day of rest?

Enrichment Options

Shabbat Mural: Have students make a Shabbat mural or collage on the theme of rest or peace. They might want to use recycled materials, things from nature, photo images, or words and phrases that reflect the value of rest. They can incorporate pictures of their families or special Shabbat items.

Shabbat Rap: Invite students to write and perform a Shabbat rap explaining the things we do on Shabbat that make it a day of rest or peace. This can include the elements we learned in this lesson, such as the blessings, the special items we use, or going to the synagogue. Alternatively, students can compose poems or songs, working individually or in small groups.

Further Resources

Visit www.behrmanhouse.com/holidays-values for links to more information on Shabbat traditions, foods, blessings, and songs.

Lesson 8: Creating Holy Time and Space

Essential Questions: How and why do we mark the transitions to and from Shabbat? What do we do on Shabbat to create holy time and space?

Goals: Students will:

1. Explain ways in which we mark transitions in life and on Shabbat.
2. Use their senses to mark the difference between the holy and the everyday.
3. Reflect on the idea of holy space and time, and how it leads to a Shabbat atmosphere.

Introduction

In life, we often mark transitions by taking action. We celebrate the New Year, we light birthday candles, we throw graduation parties, and we hold bar and bat mitzvah ceremonies. These are all transitions, and we mark them with blessings or celebrations. We also mark the transition from the regular week into Shabbat by lighting candles, reciting blessings, and sharing a special meal with family or friends. Then we mark the transition from Shabbat back to the regular week with the Havdalah ceremony.

These short, sensory actions not only provide the transition we need to acknowledge Shabbat, but they also help us to embrace the sense of peace and wholeness that we seek within ourselves on Shabbat. The activities in this lesson will focus on the value of *bein kodesh l'chol*, differentiating between the holy and the everyday, and the traditions that provide the transition we need into and out of Shabbat.

Materials Needed

- Braided Havdalah candle, matches (Get permission from the education director before lighting them.)
- Havdalah spice box and spices
- Grape juice
- Kiddush cup
- Wide rubber bands (three for each student)
- Sharpies

Activities

1. Getting Started: Making a Transition (10 minutes)

Explain that our lives are full of transitions, moments when we switch from one activity to another or even from one stage of life to another. Ask students: What are times in your day or life when you have to transition? *(possible answers: coming home after a long day at school, ending the school year and beginning the summer, having a birthday, starting a new after-school activity or sport, going to bed)*

Keep a running list of responses on the board so that students can refer to them for their journal, if they wish.

Ask students to choose a few examples of transitions, then explain what they do to mark the change. *(take off shoes and have a snack, blow out birthday candles, do warm-ups, put on pajamas, etc.)* They should write their responses in their journal, page 33. Allow a few minutes for writing and then a few minutes for students to share answers.

At the end, ask students why they think we mark transitions. (*Transitions help us move from one activity to another; they help us separate from the previous activity in order to turn our attention to the new one.*)

2. Making Meaning: Bein Kodesh L'chol (5 minutes)

Ask students how Shabbat traditions mark the transition from the regular week to Shabbat. *(They turn our attention from the week to Shabbat. All the things we do—lighting candles, eating challah, having a special meal with family and friends, going to synagogue—remind us of the difference between this day and the rest of the week.)* Explain that we ease into the holiness of Shabbat with our Friday night traditions, and we mark the transition from Shabbat back to the regular week with Havdalah, a short service that engages all our senses.

Ask a volunteer to read the phrase *bein kodesh l'chol*, "between the holy and the everyday," in the journal, page 34, and explain it in his or her own words. *(separating the sacred from the everyday, marking the transition from special back to regular)* Explain that these words come from the Havdalah blessing that we recite as Shabbat is coming to a close.

Our senses are a powerful way to feel the difference *bein kodesh l'chol.* Ask students to list things we do on Shabbat that use each of our senses to remind us of the holiness of the day. (*seeing, smelling, and feeling the warmth of candles; seeing, smelling, and tasting grape juice and challah; seeing and smelling the spice box and seeing the braided candle during Havdalah; hearing music and blessing*)

3. Have a Model Havdalah Service! (15 minutes)

As a class, model a Havdalah service. Have the class sit in a circle, pass around the grape juice, spices, and (unlit) Havdalah candle, and recite the blessings of Havdalah, found in the journal, pages 34-35. Ask students to notice how they use their senses during this short service.

Ask students to find the phrase *bein kodesh l'chol* in the blessings (twice in the last blessing), and to explain why we end Shabbat with the Havdalah service. *(It marks the transition back to the week, it reminds us of the holiness of Shabbat, it helps us take some of that holiness with us into the week, by using all our senses it fully involves us in a meaningful way.)*

4. Holy Time and Space (10 minutes)

We've talked about how Havdalah helps us separate holy time and space from the regular week. But what does *holy* mean? *(inspired by or connected to God or religion)* What is holy time? What is holy space? *(a time and place that is peaceful, special, different, good; where I can feel God's presence; where I strive to be my best self)* How does Shabbat create this atmosphere for you? Let students first enter their answers in the journal, page 36, then allow a few minutes to share.

5. Wrapping It Up: Bein Kodesh L'chol Challenge (10 minutes)

Ask students to brainstorm a list of things they can do to make their Shabbat holy. Their ideas can include anything that would help create a restful, peaceful, meaningful, or holy time and space in their lives. *(Ideas may include: spending 20 minutes completely alone, encouraging their family to light candles together, going to synagogue, spending time with a family member.)* Let students write the ideas they like best in their journal, page 36, and then choose their three favorite ideas.

Hand each student three rubber bands. Explain that they will write one of their top three ideas on each rubber band. This upcoming Shabbat, they will undertake the "*Bein Kodesh L'chol* Challenge." They are to begin Shabbat with the three bands on their left wrist. As they act on each idea, they can move that rubber band to their right wrist. Ask them to report back on the experience next week.

Enrichment Options

***B'samim* Challenge:** Tradition says that spices for Havdalah should come from the ground. But people use a wide variety of interesting things to create sweet smelling *b'samim*, spices, for Havdalah. Ask student volunteers to prepare *b'samim* for the following week to share with the class. Have students place their material in a box or envelope marked only with their name. Then, line up the samples and have students guess what each one contains, without looking. (*Materials might include: dried or fresh mint; cloves; lemon, orange, or etrog peels; flower petals; perfume; vanilla; tea leaves.*) Ask students which scents they prefer and how *b'samim* help mark the Havdalah transition.

Further Resources

Visit www.behrmanhouse.com/holidays-values for links to more Havdalah information and activities.

Lesson 9: Shabbat Shalom

Essential Questions: Why is shalom, peace, such an important part of the Shabbat experience? How can we create more shalom in ourselves, our families, and our world?

Goals: Students will:

1. Discuss different levels on which we can experience peace—within ourselves, with others, and in the world.
2. Explain how Shabbat traditions and atmosphere can help us focus on and strive for peace in our lives.
3. Define *sh'lom bayit*, the mitzvah of "peace in the home," and develop ideas to add peace to their family and Shabbat experience.

Introduction

Shalom, peace, means different things to different people. Shabbat can be a day to focus on and strive for peace in all areas of our lives—within ourselves, in our relationships with others, and in the world. In this lesson, we will focus on how to increase shalom in our lives on Shabbat and every day.

Materials Needed

- A recording of the song "Sim Shalom" (optional)

Activities

1. Getting Started: Making Meaning: Shalom (5 minutes)

Ask students when we use the word *shalom*. *(It is the word for "peace," "hello," and "goodbye"; we use it in the expressions "Shabbat shalom"—"Shabbat peace", and "Shalom Aleichem"—"peace be upon you.")* Ask students to read page 37 in the journal, and write or draw whatever thoughts or images come to mind when they think of the word *shalom*.

Take a few minutes to have students share their responses, either as a class or with a partner.

2. Shalom Inside (10 minutes)

Explain that while *shalom* means peace, the word actually comes from another word: *shaleim*, which means "whole," or "complete."

Ask students how the idea of wholeness or completeness is related to peace. *(When something or someone is missing from our life, we don't feel at peace; when we are surrounded by people and experiences that are meaningful, we do feel complete or peaceful.)*

Explain that feeling peaceful or complete inside is something we aim for, especially on Shabbat. Ask students: What are some things you do to attain a sense of peacefulness or completeness? On page 37 of the journal, ask them to fill in the peace sign with words or drawings of things they can do to feel peaceful, or a peaceful place they can go. *(my room, listening to my favorite music, reading a book, being with a friend, exercising)*

3. Values in Action: Sh'lom Bayit (20 minutes)

Part of observing Shabbat is creating a peaceful time and space. We try to do this at the synagogue, with friends, and especially in our homes. This value is called *sh'lom bayit.*

Pair students with *chevruta* partners and ask them to work together to make up stories about *sh'lom bayit* based on the photos in the journal, page 38, or to share real-life stories of *sh'lom bayit* from their own lives. Then ask for volunteers to share one of their stories with the class.

Discuss:

- How can Shabbat help us increase *sh'lom bayit* in our lives? *(Families may spend more time together on Shabbat; a day of rest can be peaceful; building sh'lom bayit can strengthen our relationships with each other; we work to create a space that is peaceful, restful, or safe; a peaceful world begins in the home, then we can spread or expand the value to others.)*
- What are some things you can do to share Shabbat peace with your family? *(help a younger sibling get dressed or read a book together; choose a specific Shabbat-related activity to do with a parent, like lighting candles or baking challah)*

4. Sim Shalom (10 minutes)

Turn to page 39 in the journal and sing together the song "Sim Shalom," or invite the cantor to come teach it to the class. As an alternative, play a recording of it quietly in the room as students reflect on and discuss the meaning of the prayer. (Visit www.behrmanhouse.com/holidays-values for a link to the song.)

Ask students to read the prayer in English, then write in their journals or discuss:

- What is the poet praying for? *(peace for us and for all the people of Israel)*
- What are the ingredients for peace as described in this prayer? *(Torah, love, kindness, righteousness, blessing, mercy, life)*
- What do you think is necessary for a peaceful world?
- What can you do to create more peace in your life, your home, the world?

5. Wrapping It Up (5 minutes)

Remind students that Shabbat is about creating holy and peaceful time and space. Ask students to commit to trying something new this Shabbat that will help create a holy, peaceful, restful time and space. *(Ideas might include saying a newly learned blessing, turning off computers and phones, lighting candles, telling stories with family members, inviting friends to share a meal, helping siblings.)* Remind students that the most important element is welcoming in the precious time, and creating a space that is peaceful and open.

Enrichment Options

Shalom Means Knowing Your Neighbors: The concept of shalom doesn't begin and end with Shabbat. We should aim for peace and wholeness every day. And while peace begins in the home (*sh'lom bayit*), it should be the goal of all people and nations. We can start by getting to know our neighbors better. Plan a meeting or a pen pal or Skype session with a class from a neighboring church group or mosque. Have students prepare questions in advance to ask the children, in order to get to know them a little. Prepare questions beforehand on the topic of their Sabbath or day of rest. *(Do you have a Sabbath? When is it? What do you do? What things do you and your community pray for on the Sabbath?)* Afterwards discuss how doing this brings peace into the world.

Further Resources

Visit www.behrmanhouse.com/holidays-values for links to activities, songs, and other resources about Shabbat.

Chapter

5

HANUKKAH

Courage • *Gevurah*

On Hanukkah, we celebrate the courage of the Maccabees, who rebelled against the Syrians and stood up for what they believed in. What can we learn from the Maccabees in today's world, when we enjoy religious freedom and relative security? In this chapter, we explore different ways we can learn from the Maccabees and act courageously.

In lesson 10, we discuss the story of the Maccabees and the courage that they showed by fighting back against the powerful Syrian army. In lesson 11, we explore what the traditions of Hanukkah teach us about courage today, as we look at examples of courage from modern Jewish history and in our own lives. In lesson 12, we challenge the traditional understanding of courage and suggest that courage comes in many different forms. A soldier who leaves his family to go fight in a war is courageous, but so is the friend who struggles not to let his or her anger or fear get the best of him or her, or the student who stands up to a bully.

Lesson 10: Courage of the Maccabees

Essential Question: How can the value of courage, which we learn from the story of the Maccabees, help us to be better people?

Goals: Students will:

1. Understand how to light a *hanukkiyah*, a Hanukkah menorah, and the meaning behind it.
2. Define *gevurah*, "courage," and give examples of ways that people demonstrate this value.
3. Compare and contrast *gevurah* in the Hanukkah story with courage in present-day life.

Introduction

The First Book of the Maccabees describes the Maccabean Revolt against King Antiochus IV Epiphanes. Upon the death of his father, Mattathias, Judah led the Jews to victory, rededicating the Second Temple in Jerusalem in 165 BCE and establishing the Hanukkah holiday. There are four Books of the Maccabees, none of which mentions the miracle of the oil, which many of us associate with Hanukkah. The miracle of the oil was first discussed in the Babylonian Talmud many years later as the reason that we light candles on Hanukkah. It is possible that the rabbis, religious leaders living in exile from Israel under the rule of others, wished to emphasize the spiritual miracle rather than the military miracle of Jews fighting for their independence in Israel, which was less relevant to them at the time.

On Hanukkah, we celebrate the courage of the Maccabees, who rebelled against the powerful Syrians and stood up for what they believed in, even when doing so was very dangerous. What can we, living in twenty-first-century North America, where we enjoy freedom of religion and relative security, learn from the courage of the Maccabees when they rebelled against the Syrians? Or would we prefer to focus our celebration of Hanukkah on the spiritual victory of the miracle of the oil?

Materials Needed

- Markers or colored pencils for illustrating *gevurah*
- Access to the Internet and a printer to print out images, or magazines and newspapers from which the students can cut out images

Activities

1. Getting Started: Who Are Your Heroes? (10 minutes)

Ask students to write privately about heroes and courage on page 40 of the journal. Tell students that a hero can be someone they know personally—a family member, friend, or community member—or someone they know about from history or current events.

If there's time, students can share their answers with a partner.

2. What Is the Miracle of Hanukkah? (15 minutes)

Ask students to read page 41 in the journal and think about these questions: Which miracle is the most relevant for us as Jews living in twenty-first-century America? Should we emphasize the story of the Maccabees who fought for their beliefs and won an astounding military victory? Or should we emphasize the spiritual victory of the oil?

Divide the students into two groups. One group prepares an argument for why we should celebrate the Maccabean victory over the Syrians, and the second group prepares an argument for why we should celebrate the miracle of the oil. Each group presents their arguments and answers questions from the other side. If possible, invite someone to come in to the classroom and serve as the judge. Alternatively, ask the students to vote.

At the end of the debate, discuss how both fighting the Syrians and lighting the Menorah showed courage. *(The courageous Maccabees risked their lives to fight the Syrians, even though the Syrians had more soldiers and better weapons. The Maccabees also had the courage to light the Menorah, to have hope for the future, and to stay strong in their beliefs even though it seemed like there was no chance the oil would last. The first act demonstrated physical courage; the second act demonstrated spiritual courage.)*

3. Human Menorah (10 minutes)

Invite the students to create a human menorah following the directions in the journal on page 42. As each candles is "lit," students finish the sentence "I would stand up for…" (*Possible responses include: I would stand up for the right to practice Judaism freely, I would stand up for my family and friends if they were in trouble, I would stand up for Israel.*)

Then practice the blessings to be said at home when the menorah is lit.

Visit www.behrmanhouse.com/holidays-values for directions on how to light the menorah.

4. Wrapping It Up: Making Meaning: Gevurah (10 minutes)

Write the word *gevurah* on the board, and define it as "courage." Point out that the Hebrew word for "hero," *gibor,* comes from the same root. Ask students what they think it means to be a *gibor,* to show courage. Encourage them to discuss this with a partner and then, individually or together, illustrate their responses on page 43 using images, symbols, or cartoons.

Advance preparation for Lesson 12: Ask students to interview family members at home and record a story of courage about someone in their family. Students should write or record the story and bring it to school along with a photo of the person for the third lesson in the Hanukkah chapter (Lesson 12, Activity 4).

Enrichment Options

Greeks, Syrians, or Seleucids: The Maccabees rebelled against the Seleucids, who conquered the Holy Land in the third century BCE. The Seleucids are often referred to as Greeks, even though they were actually from Syria, because they spread Hellenistic (Greek) religion and culture. We refer to them as Syrians in this book. Like the Syrians, many Jews wanted to become Hellenists and participate in Greek cultural activities, such as the theater or the Olympics (the Greeks valued athleticism and celebrated the beauty of the human body). Some Jews viewed participation in these activities as a waste of time and an effort to assimilate into Greek culture. Ask students to debate: If you were a Jew at that time, would you have participated in the Olympics and gone to the theater? Why or why not?

Rededication of the Temple (*Hanukkat Habayit*): Hanukkah celebrates the rededication of the Temple in Jerusalem by the Maccabees in 165 BCE. Ask students to silently mime the reactions of the Maccabees when they entered the Temple that had been desecrated by the Greeks. You can award points or small prizes for the most expressive mime.

Fried Foods: Explain to the class that we light the *hanukkiyah* and eat foods fried in oil, such as latkes (potato pancakes), to celebrate the miracle of the oil. With permission from the education director, bring in latkes or another food fried in oil (such as *sufganiyot,* jelly doughnuts). If you have access to a kitchen, make latkes together. Or bring in a variety of foods and experiment with frying them. As you eat the fried foods, discuss with your class what gave the Maccabees the courage to light the Menorah even when there was only enough oil for one day.

Lesson 11: Today's Maccabees

Essential Question: What are examples of *gevurah* today, in modern Jewish history and in our lives?

Goals: Students will:

1. Discuss what the traditions of Hanukkah teach us about courage today.
2. Give examples of *gevurah* from modern Jewish history.
3. Reflect on opportunities in their own lives to stand up for their beliefs and declare their pride in being Jewish.

Introduction

In the popular Hanukkah song "Mi Y'maleil" we sing, "In every age, a hero or sage came to our aid." Who are the Maccabees of modern Jewish history? We often focus on the courage of those who fought for the Jewish state—the pioneers, soldiers in Israel's War of Independence and subsequent wars. But we can also focus on a different kind of courage—the courage to stand up for your beliefs and do something different than everyone else, even when it is difficult and scary. We celebrate both kinds of courage when we light the *hanukkiyah* and declare our pride in being Jewish.

Materials Needed

- Internet access or printouts describing modern Jewish heroes
- Optional: arts and crafts materials and poster board

Activities

1. Getting Started: What Would You Do? (10 minutes)

Ask students to read the dilemma in their journal, page 44, and respond privately. Invite students to share their responses with the class, making sure to include different points of view.

Of course some of the students will say that they would choose to play the game—but others might say that they wouldn't play. The point of the exercise is to discuss openly the question and get kids thinking, and ideally for the kids to hear from their friends why Yom Kippur might just be important enough to give up the game.

Tell students about Sandy Koufax, who chose not to play on Yom Kippur in the 1965 World Series. More recently, in 2004, Kevin Youkilis sat out a Boston Red Sox game on Yom Kippur (though he did sit in the dugout in his uniform), and in 2012, when Youkilis was playing for the Chicago White Sox, a game was moved from 7:10 pm to 1:10 pm so as not to conflict with Yom Kippur. Ask students: What do you think of these decisions? Encourage students to think about how it might take courage to make a decision like this.

2. Singing Together: "Mi Y'maleil" (10 minutes)

As a class, learn the words to this popular Hanukkah song and sing it together in English (page 45) and Hebrew. For fun, try to sing it in a round. See www.behrmanhouse.com/holidays-values for a link to the tune and the Hebrew words.

Discuss:

- Remind students about the debate during the last lesson. According to this song, what do we celebrate on Hanukkah? (*This song focuses on the courage of the Maccabees rather than the miracle of the oil.)*
- This song was written by Menashe Rabina, a Zionist who made *aliyah* in the early twentieth century. Why do you think many Israeli songs focus on the military victory and the Maccabees' courage? (*Israelis often make a connection between the Maccabees' military victory and the Jewish victory in the Israeli War of Independence. In both cases, small Jewish armies defeated their much more powerful enemies in order to declare an independent Jewish state.)*

3. Values in Action: "In Every Age, a Hero or Sage" (25 minutes)

Divide students into small groups. Each group chooses a modern hero who rose up to save the Jewish people. (See pages 46-47 of the journal for some examples, but encourage students to consider other heroes, too). Students research that person on the Internet. If you do not have Internet access, print out one-page biographies of different heroes for the students to choose from. (See www.behrmanhouse.com/holidays-values for links to some biographies).

Encourage each group to use a creative medium—a short skit, PowerPoint presentation, song, poem, poster, newspaper article, etc.— to teach the rest of the class about the person they chose, with a focus on what makes this person a hero. Then let each group present to the class.

You may choose to expand this exercise to include other modern-day heroes, not only those who rose up to save the Jewish people.

4. Wrapping It Up: Jewish Pride (5 minutes)

While traditionally the celebration of Hanukkah focuses on the Maccabees, we can also see Hanukkah as a celebration of everyday courage by ordinary people like you and me.

Ask students to respond privately to the prompts on page 47 of the journal. If there's time, students can share some part of what they wrote with a partner.

Lesson 12: Who Is Courageous?

Essential Question: What are different ways of being courageous?

Goals: Students will:

1. Explore what the Hanukkah traditions teach us about different kinds of *gevurah.*
2. Compare and contrast different kinds of *gevurah.*
3. Reflect personally on how they are or wish to be courageous in their own lives.

Introduction

The rabbis, based on a verse from Proverbs, complicate our understanding of courage, arguing that it is more courageous to have self-control than to conquer a city. In other words, it often takes more courage to fight the battles within ourselves than to fight an external enemy. You don't have to be famous or physically strong to be courageous. Each of us is courageous every time we make a choice to overcome our own fears, anger, or social pressure. On Hanukkah, when we light the candles, eat latkes, and play dreidel, we are celebrating this everyday courage as well.

Materials Needed

- Dreidels and Hanukkah *gelt*
- Arts and crafts materials for creating an exhibition
- Computer with printer
- Family interviews, from end of Lesson 10

Advance Preparation

Write each of the four captions from page 49 of the journal on a separate paper (for Activity 2, below).

Activities

1. Getting Started: Playing Dreidel (5 minutes)

Ask a volunteer to read the paragraph on page 48 of the journal out loud. Students should respond to the question privately. If there's time, either at the beginning or end of class, students can play dreidel.

Visit www.behrmanhouse.com/holidays-values for directions on how to play dreidel.

2. Values in Action: Courage in Our World Today (10 minutes)

Ask students to look at the images from page 49 of the journal. Post the image captions (see Advance Preparation) around the room. Ask students to identify how each of these people is showing courage. Then ask students to choose which one they relate to the most, by going to stand near that caption. Ask students to give examples from their own lives to explain why these acts are courageous. If most students chose the more obvious images, challenge them to explain why someone would choose the less obvious images—

such as taking a deep breath to calm down before you say something you regret.

Here are some questions to get students thinking about the nature of courage:

- Is courage only about facing our fear of physical danger? What other kinds of fears can we face? (*fear that people won't like me, fear of change)*
- Which takes more courage—doing something that everyone else is doing, even though it may be dangerous (such as defending your country in the army), or doing something different from everyone else, such as standing up to a bully when no one else will?
- Note that the rabbis say: "Who is a hero among heroes? . . . Someone who makes their enemy their friend." (*Avot de Rabbi Natan*) According to this quote, which act on page 49 is the most courageous? Do you agree? Why or why not?

3. Who Is Courageous? (15 minutes)

Together read the teaching from *Pirkei Avot* in the Student Journal, page 50. Ask students to explain the teaching in their own words. Then have students discuss the question beneath the quote.

Explain that *gevurah* can also be translated more simply as "strength," and can include everyday acts such as studying hard for a test when you would rather be hanging out with your friends, or helping out a friend who is going through a difficult time. Ask: Can you think of examples of *gevurah,* strength, from your own life?

As students may already have pointed out, being courageous is not a competition. There are many different types of courage, and one kind of courage is not necessarily better than another. But in the teaching from *Pirkei Avot*, the rabbis of the Mishnah seem to make courage into a competition. Why? (*Perhaps the rabbis want to give us an ideal of courage that is within our reach. We may not all be able to conquer a city—especially in the times of the rabbis, when there was no Jewish army—but we can all try not to get angry and say something we regret.)*

Ask students to respond to the journal prompt privately.

4. Wrapping It Up: Collage of Courage (20 minutes)

Ask students to make a collage of different images of courage. Encourage students to include many different kinds of courage. They might want to include the following:

- Images from the Hanukkah story
- Student projects about heroes in modern times
- Quotes from each student, "I was courageous when…," and photos of the different students in your class (not necessarily matched with the quotes—students may prefer that the quotes remain anonymous)
- Photos and stories of courage from family members whom the students interviewed earlier in Lesson 10, following Activity 4

Make an exhibition of students' collages, and invite other students in the school and family members to view the exhibition.

Chapter

6

TU BISHEVAT

Caring for the Environment • *Bal Tashchit*

Tu BiShevat is often referred to as "the New Year of the Trees." Historically, it was the date on which our ancestors counted the years of a tree's life in order to fulfill laws about eating or tithing the fruit to the Temple. But it has evolved into a holiday that celebrates the environment. On this holiday, we are reminded of the importance of taking care of the earth, as we are charged to do in Genesis 2:15: "The Lord God took the man and placed him in the garden of Eden, to till it and tend it." In addition, we honor the idea of *bal tashchit,* avoiding wastefulness and using our resources responsibly. We not only recognize the importance of trees in ancient Israel and in our lives today, but also appreciate the constant cycle of nature and living things all over the world.

In this chapter, students will bring Tu BiShevat to the classroom in a relevant and exciting way. In lesson 13, we will learn ways in which we are commanded as Jews to protect our world for ourselves and for those who come after us. In lesson 14, we will delve into the value of *bal tashchit* and apply it to our own lives by developing an action plan.

Lesson 13: We Are Guardians

Essential Question: How does Tu BiShevat guide us in making decisions to help protect the environment for future generations?

Goals: Students will:

1. Explain the connection between Tu BiShevat and the cycles of growth on earth.
2. Examine ways in which our Jewish heritage and texts can teach us lessons today about protecting natural resources.
3. Discuss the Jewish value of seeing oneself as a guardian of our natural world.

Introduction

On Tu BiShevat, we celebrate the beginning of a new growing cycle of trees. Many people celebrate by tasting a variety of fruits that typically grow in Israel, or by donating money for trees to be planted in Israel. One of the most unique aspects of Tu BiShevat is that it is a holiday that not only celebrates growing, but has itself grown and changed throughout Jewish history. Traditions have been added, such as the Tu BiShevat seder, at which we say different blessings over different fruits, depending on how they each grow. Another modern custom is to focus on projects that improve the environment or help protect natural resources.

For this lesson, students will learn the basics about Tu BiShevat as well as develop an understanding of how important trees are in our lives. Students will come to understand that as Jews, we are commanded to protect our world for ourselves and for those who come after us.

Materials Needed

- Paper
- Colored pencils
- Almonds, figs, a pomegranate, raisins, dates, or other dried fruits and nuts. Bring enough of each food to give each student a sample. (Be sure to check first with the education director about synagogue rules regarding keeping kosher and allergies.)

Activities

1. Getting Started: Happy New Year!? (5 minutes)

Ask students to respond to the journal prompts on page 51. Let students share their responses in pairs or with the class, if they choose.

2. The Old Man and the Carob Tree (10 minutes)

Central to Tu BiShevat is the idea that humans are guardians over the world for the generations that come after us. This is a very powerful statement. The story of the old man and the carob tree reflects that value and is a great way to open the lesson.

Ask students to read the story on page 52 of the journal, then discuss the questions below. Give students a few minutes to answer the questions in their journals if you wish.

Discuss the following as a class or in groups:

- What is this story trying to tell us? Why read it on Tu BiShevat? *(to show that we are all responsible for the environment, what we do today affects the future, the story reflects the values that we focus on during Tu BiShevat)*
- Our tradition says we are supposed to be guardians over the world for future generations. What does this mean? *(A guardian is someone who watches over something and protects it. By recycling, reducing waste, and carpooling, we are watching over the world and making sure our children and grandchildren have a healthy environment in which to live.)*
- Why should we care about future generations?
- What things do you or your family do to help guard or protect the earth for the future?

3. Why Celebrate Trees? (10 minutes)

Explain to your students that Tu BiShevat, known as "The Birthday of the Trees," provides a time and a way to celebrate not only trees, but also other gifts that nature gives us. Tu BiShevat is celebrated in the winter because that's the time when the first trees in Israel blossom. We celebrate it by being outdoors (if it's warm enough, which it is in Israel), tasting varieties of fruits and tree nuts or having a Tu BiShevat seder, and by learning about and thanking God for the cycles in nature that help trees to grow. There are even different blessings for different varieties of foods.

Pass out fruits and nuts for students to try. You can find the appropriate blessings at www.behrmanhouse.com/holidays-values. While they are eating, ask: Why are trees a gift? Invite students to write in their journals (page 53) things that trees do for us and for the world, beyond the obvious answers of providing fruit and lumber. You can have them share their thoughts and create a class list on the board. Ask students to choose one item that they feel is most important and explain why.

Some possible responses for what trees do for us and for the world:

- Purify the air
- Produce oxygen
- Provide paper
- Provide medicine, food, sap, gum
- Provide shade
- Provide homes for birds, insects, animals
- Act as windbreakers
- Beautify the land
- Anchor the soil to prevent erosion

4. Tree Observation (20 minutes)

Explain to your students that it's hard to really appreciate something without taking a more careful look. Take your students outside to observe a tree. Encourage them to sit quietly and observe deeply, with several of their senses. Then they can write or draw their observations on page 54 of their journal.

5. Wrapping It Up (5 minutes)

Tell students that historically Tu BiShevat was the date on which our ancestors counted the years of a tree's life in order to fulfill laws about eating or giving fruit to the Temple. Ask students why they think it has evolved into a holiday that celebrates the environment. Why do we need a holiday for that?

Enrichment Options

Puzzle Time: The Seven Species
A quick crossword with clues to the seven species will give students a "taste" of the varieties traditionally celebrated.

Answers:

Across
4. Pomegranate
6. Fig
7. Grape

Down
1. Barley
2. Wheat
3. (Date) palm
5. Olive

Sing about It: Together with the class, learn "Hashkeidiyah Porachat," a classic Tu BiShevat song in Israel. The title means "The Almond Tree Is Blooming." Visit www.behrmanhouse.com/holidays-values for a link to the song.

Lesson 14: *Bal Tashchit,* or "Reduce, Reuse, Recycle"

Essential Questions: What is the value of *bal tashchit* and how does it relate to Tu BiShevat? How do our everyday actions and choices affect the world?

Goals: Students will:

1. Define the value of *bal tashchit* as the idea of limiting excess waste and not using materials carelessly.
2. Explain how Tu BiShevat reminds us that our actions have consequences.

Introduction

The idea of *bal tashchit* reminds us to limit excess waste and not use materials carelessly. We can practice this value all year long, but it's especially relevant to remember on Tu BiShevat, when we celebrate trees. The commandment *bal tashchit* prohibits us from destroying trees, and, by extension, teaches us to be aware of and responsible for our environment, and all of our natural resources. In this lesson, students will have the opportunity to connect this value to their own lives and actions.

Materials Needed

- Pencils and paper
- Optional: poster board, art supplies

Advance Preparation

Invite the education director to visit the class near the end of the lesson to see and hear students' presentations about promoting *bal tashchit* in the school.

Activities

1. Getting Started: Making Meaning: Bal Tashchit (5 minutes)

Remind students that in Lesson 13, we learned what Tu BiShevat is and we talked about being guardians of the world. We also listed reasons why trees are so important to us and to the world.

Bal tashchit, in English "do not destroy," is a commandment from the Torah that prohibits us from wasting or destroying anything without reason. Ask a student to read aloud the prohibition (from Deuteronomy 20:19-20) in the journal, page 56. Then ask for a volunteer to explain the prohibition. *(You are not allowed to destroy fruit trees, even if you have captured a city during a war.)* Explain that later, rabbis interpreted this verse to apply at all times, not just in times of war, and not just with trees.

Why is this ancient commandment important to remember in our world today? *(As our world gets more crowded and we use up more and more resources, it's more important than ever to avoid waste and to conserve limited resources, such as oil; to reduce pollution; and to preserve endangered species.)*

2. Bal Tashchit Game (15 minutes)

Divide the students into small groups and have them play a Pictionary-style *bal tashchit* drawing game, as described in the journal on page 57. Let them play for 10 minutes, until you're sure they have a solid idea of the concept and how it relates to their lives.

Ask a volunteer from each group to share some of their ideas with the class. The discussion might include the following:

- Use less gas by carpooling.
- Use both sides of a sheet of paper.
- Buy things with less packaging.
- Don't throw out edible food.
- Avoid using limited or endangered resources (such as animal furs and skins).
- Recycle trash whenever possible.
- Compost food waste.
- Donate used clothing or other items.
- Buy local or organic foods and other products.
- Choose to receive electronic bills instead of paper.

Discuss: How does Tu BiShevat remind us of the value of *bal tashchit*? (*On Tu BiShevat we celebrate trees, and bal tashchit is based on a commandment about not destroying fruit trees; both are about respecting and caring for the earth; Tu BiShevat has become an environmental-themed holiday in recent years.*)

3. Try This: Carbon Footprint (5 minutes)

Challenge students to measure their carbon footprint, or impact on the environment. Visit www.behrmanhouse.com/holidays-values for a link to a carbon footprint calculator, as well as more ways to reduce waste and avoid destroying natural resources.

4. Making It happen: A Tu BiShevat Proposal (20 minutes)

Organize your students into groups of three or four. Ask each group to create a proposal (following the prompts on page 58) suggesting something the school can do to promote *bal tashchit* on Tu BiShevat and throughout the year. Remind students they can refer to the ideas on the board from the previous discussion. The proposal can be in the form of a letter to the education director, a skit, a poster, a PowerPoint, a song, or any other creative idea. It should include the following:

- A short explanation of the value of *bal tashchit*
- A brief description of the group's idea and how it can help the environment
- An explanation of why Tu BiShevat is a good time to implement this idea
- A plan for how the group can carry out their idea

Invite the education director to visit the class for presentations. Have each group present their idea and take questions from the director, the rest of the class, or you. As a class, discuss whether the ideas are feasible, and how students can work on them during the duration of the school year, as a long-term project.

5. Wrapping It Up: Acting on Bal Tashchit (5 minutes)

After your students present, wrap up the lesson by reminding them that living the value of *bal tashchit* takes determination and thoughtfulness, and sometimes a great deal of time. Ask students to read the quote from *Pirkei Avot* on page 58 of the journal and discuss: What does this mean for our class? *(While we have amazing ideas, we may not be able to put all of them into action. But we're still obligated to do what we can.)*

Enrichment Options

Environmental Organizations: Find out about Jewish National Fund, an organization that works to protect and revitalize Israel's natural environment. Write about one project they do, why it's important, and how it connects to the two values discussed in this chapter: being a guardian of our world's resources, and not producing excess waste. Include one way that students can help or become involved. Then, do it!

Alternatively, you can visit the U.S. Environmental Protection Agency's website. Students can click on their state and see what is happening in their own backyards. Have kids compare and contrast projects on both websites to see different things happening to make the world a little more "green." Find links to these organizations in the Further Resources section, below.

Electricity Tally: Who turned out the lights? The Jewish Climate Initiative website gives a great explanation of *bal tashchit* and all of the ways we can avoid harming our world. Encourage students to keep a tally of how many lights are on in their house at a given time. Ask them to report their tallies each week for a few weeks in a row, reminding them that using more electricity than needed wastes resources. Keep a record of how the numbers change (or don't change, but let's hope they do!).

Learn a New Song: "Tzadik Katamar"
Tzadik katamar yifrach yifrach, tzadik katamar yifrach (2x)
K'erez bal'vanon yisgeh (2x)
K'erez bal'vanon yisgeh yisgeh.
"The righteous will flourish like a date palm and grow tall like a cedar in Lebanon."
(Psalms 92:13)

Further Resources

Visit www.behrmanhouse.com/holidays-values for more information on connecting environmentalism and Judaism, as well as links to books and websites with ideas for getting involved, reducing waste, having a Tu BiShevat Seder, and more. You will also find links to Jewish National Fund, the U.S. Environmental Protection Agency, and the Jewish Climate Initiative.

Chapter

7

PURIM

Justice • *Tzedek*, and Giving • *Tzedakah*

Purim is a holiday that originated after the time of the Torah. On Purim, we read *Megillat Esther*, the scroll that tells the story of how Esther and Mordecai saved the Jews of Shushan from persecution. We celebrate the victory of the Jewish community by rejoicing in a festive and lighthearted way. Children (and sometimes adults) dress in costume; we use noisemakers, called *graggers*, to drown out the name of the evil Haman. On Purim, we are commanded to give gifts of food to friends and family, and tzedakah to those in need.

In lesson 15, we will study the reasons we give to others, by making *mishlo'ach manot* (gifts of food for friends and family) and giving tzedakah, called *matanot la'evyonim,* to those in need. In lesson 16, we will examine the value of *tzedek*, "justice," through the lens of Esther and Mordecai's actions, and we will ask ourselves what injustices exist in the world today and how we can stand up for what is right, as our ancestors did so long ago.

Lesson 15: Giving and Tzedakah

Essential Questions: Why do people give to others? How do the story and themes of Purim encourage us to give to others—both to friends and to those in need?

Goals: Students will:

1. Understand the main practices and traditions of Purim.
2. Create *mishlo'ach manot* baskets for friends and family members.
3. Explain the commandment to give tzedakah—*matanot la'evyonim*—to the poor, on Purim.

Introduction

One of the key *mitzvot* we are commanded to perform on Purim is giving tzedakah. We are also commanded to give *mishlo'ach manot*, gifts of food to friends and family. These customs come from the verse in the *megillah* that says, "...They were to observe them as days of feasting and merrymaking, and as an occasion for sending gifts to one another and presents to the poor." (Esther 9:22) We are obligated to give these gifts on the actual day of Purim.

For this lesson, students will investigate the reasons people give, and why it is commanded on Purim. They will help prepare *mishlo'ach manot* for friends and family members, and they will give *matanot la'evyonim* to those in need.

Materials Needed

- *Megillah*, or photo of a *megillah*
- Food for *mishlo'ach manot* bags. This can include *hamantashen*, fruit, nuts, or candies. Each bag should have at least two edible treats.
- Bags or baskets
- Optional: a small toy or something for a child such as bubbles or a yo-yo

Advance Preparation

See if your school will provide the foods and bags or baskets needed for creating *mishlo'ach manot*, or ask students in advance to bring in their contributions.

Activities

1. Getting Started: Making a Difference (5 minutes)

Ask students to respond to the journal prompt on page 59 of the journal.

2. Megillat Esther: The Megillah (5 minutes)

Explain to students that we're commanded to do four mitzvot on Purim. The first is to hear the reading of

Megillat Esther, the scroll that tells the story of Purim. The second mitzvah is to eat, drink, and be merry. (We will come back to the third and fourth *mitzvot* later in this lesson.)

Show students a *Megillat Esther*, or a photo of a *megillah*, and ask: How is this *megillah* similar to a Torah scroll? (*it's written on a roll of parchment, it's part of the Bible*) How is it different? (*it is smaller; has just one roller; it only contains one book, the Book of Esther*) What happens in the synagogue when the megillah is read? (*we drown out Haman's name with noisemakers and booing*) What are some other customs related to Purim? (*we dress up in costumes, have a Purim carnival, eat hamantashen*)

3. The Purim Story (15 minutes)

Ask a student to read aloud the story on page 60 of the journal. Have students fill in their responses to the questions that follow. Discuss as a class.

4. Making Meaning: Tzedakah (5 minutes)

Ask students to read the definition of tzedakah in the journal, page 62. Explain that tzedakah is not simply "charity," as it's sometimes translated. It is a commandment to give to those in need because it's the right thing to do.

5. The Mitzvah of Giving (15 minutes)

The third and fourth commandments on Purim involve giving. We are commanded to give *matanot la'evyonim*, gifts to the poor, and *mishlo'ach manot*, gifts of food, often including *hamantashen*, to family and friends.

Ask students to think about how giving strengthens a community. (*builds friendships, helps those in need, brings us together for a common purpose*)

What are some other reasons we give, whether gifts to friends or tzedakah to those in need? Let students respond to the prompts on pages 62-63 in their journal, then ask for volunteers to share with the class. *(Responses may include: the Torah commands us to give tzedakah; we give tzedakah to help those in need, to connect with our community, to correct an injustice, to make a difference in the world, to feel good about ourselves; we give gifts to make our families or friends feel good.)* Ask: How does it feel to give? Are your answers different depending on the type of gift (*matanot la'evyonim* or *mishlo'ach manot*)?

Distribute materials and let students make their own *mishlo'ach manot* gift bag or basket to give to a friend or family member. Prompt students to include a Purim card in which they state three reasons why they are giving this gift *(because you're my friend, because I know you like hamantashen, because it's fun to give mishlo'ach manot, etc.)*.

6. Wrapping It Up: Values in Action: Tzedakah around the World (5 minutes)

Pair students in *chevruta*, and ask each student to choose one of the images on page 64 of the journal, explaining to their partner this religion's attitude toward giving.

Ask why tzedakah and similar values are found in all major religions. (*Religions are concerned with helping others, with our spiritual lives, and with supporting the community; giving strengthens community by building our connections with one another.*)

Enrichment Options

Eight Levels of Tzedakah: Maimonides, a twelfth-century rabbi, philosopher, and commentator, identified and described eight levels of tzedakah, each one greater than the one below it. Study the eight levels, differentiating between each one by coming up with examples together. Discuss the differences between each and why Maimonides ordered them the way he did. Into which level do *mishlo'ach manot* and *matanot la'evyonim* fit? (Visit www.behrmanhouse.com/holidays-values for a link to the eight levels.)

Class Tzedakah Project: Explain that tzedakah is a value that is mentioned in *Megillat Esther* but can be performed any—and all—the time. You may have heard that many kids choose a tzedakah project for their bar or bat mitzvah. But you don't have to wait until then. Brainstorm with the students a few ideas for class tzedakah projects. (*Some ideas might include collecting shoes for children in need, collecting Purim gifts for Israeli soldiers, or collecting pajamas and books for children.*) Consider: How will you collect the items and distribute them? Will you get others involved? How can you be helpful without giving money (or asking parents to give money)? What is your goal? How will you and your class carry it out?

Further Resources

Visit www.behrmanhouse.com/holidays-values for more information on tzedakah and class projects.

Lesson 16: Justice, Justice You Shall Pursue

Essential Questions: What is justice, and why do people put themselves at risk to fight for it? How do the main characters in the Purim story serve as examples of justice?

Goals: Students will:

1. Explain how Esther and Mordecai risked their lives to fight for justice for their people.
2. Understand that there are injustices in the world and that there are many ways to respond to them.

Introduction

In the Purim story, Queen Esther fights to save her fellow Jews. She approaches King Ahasuerus in order to reveal Haman's plot, even when doing so could cost her her life. Mordecai also stands up for justice—by not bowing down to Haman and by encouraging Esther to intervene with the king. This lesson will examine the value of *tzedek*, "justice," and look at examples of justice in this story, in our history, and in our lives today.

Advance Preparation

Optional: Write each of the three captions from page 66 of the journal on a separate paper (for Activity 2, below).

Activities

1. Getting Started: Making Meaning: Tzedek (10 minutes)

Remind students that in the last lesson, we studied the story of Purim and the value of tzedakah. Now, looking at justice, or *tzedek*, your students may notice how similar these words are. First, ask students what justice is and record some of their answers on the board. Then, ask them to look at page 65 in their journal and compare these two words. Ask students what they notice about the two words. Circle the letters they have in common. Ask students why they think these two words are similar in Hebrew. (If they are interested, refer them to the Did You Know about root letters, also on page 65.)

The Torah provides plenty of material on the value of *tzedek*. Ask students to find the phrase *Tzedek, tzedek tirdof* in Deuteronomy 16:20. Discuss: Why is the word *tzedek* repeated? Why must we pursue justice, and how have different cultures done that?

2. Values in Action: Pursuing Justice (15 minutes)

Ask students to look carefully at each of the images on page 66 of their journal, thinking about what is happening and how it shows an example of someone standing up for justice. Give students time to respond to the prompts, then allow some time to share responses.

Alternatively, post the image captions (see Advance Preparation) on different walls of the room. Ask students to go around the room and write next to each caption their thoughts about how the people in the image are demonstrating *tzedek*.

3. Tzedek Today (15 minutes)

As a class, brainstorm injustices we see today. This can include anything from homelessness to a student being treated unfairly at school. Keep a list on the board as students share ideas. Ask students, in pairs, to fill in the chart in their journal, page 67, explaining injustices (either those brainstormed together or other ideas they have) and ideas for what they could do to right them. They can include drawings and other details explaining where and why the injustice occurs. Prompt them to be creative and think deeply about what they can do individually to address injustice, and how they can speak out to encourage others to address injustice in the world.

4. Wrapping It Up (5 minutes)

Close by asking whether justice, *tzedek*, always prevails. Why or why not? The Purim story is an example of justice prevailing, but are there examples in Jewish history where justice has failed? *(the Holocaust, the Spanish Inquisition, destruction of the Temple)* How does acting on behalf of justice make students feel? *(scared, worried, excited, nervous, hopeful)*

Enrichment Options

Mask of Justice: Have students create Purim masks representing the actions of Mordecai and Esther. Brainstorm words that describe the personalities of Esther and Mordecai as they acted for justice. Provide art materials and have students decorate their masks with these words and related images.

Further Resources

Visit www.behrmanhouse.com/holidays-values for links to information on masks and the Purim story.

Chapter 8

PASSOVER

Loving the Stranger • *Ahavat Hager*

The Passover haggadah tells us: "In every generation, each of us must see ourselves as if we personally went out of Egypt." The seder is full of strategies to help us make the memory of the Exodus come alive. But why is it so important to see ourselves as if we were liberated from Egypt? Jewish tradition teaches us that if we internalize the experience of slavery—if we really know what it means to be oppressed and persecuted—we will have empathy for others in difficult situations, and we will act to help them. The Torah commands us over and over again to love the stranger as ourselves, for we, too, were once strangers in Egypt.

In this chapter, we will explore how the holiday of Passover can motivate us to become more empathetic people, people who help the stranger—the weak, the vulnerable, and the different—in our communities and around the world. In Lesson 17, we will explore how the Passover seder helps us to experience what it was like to be a slave in Egypt. Lesson 18 will introduce the mitzvah of *ahavat hager,* "loving the stranger," and explore what it means to help the stranger in our schools and communities. In Lesson 19 we will apply this mitzvah on a more global level, giving students the opportunity to design and execute a social justice project to help the strangers in our world today.

Lesson 17: Seeing Myself as if I Went Out of Egypt

Essential Questions: How can we, living in relative freedom and prosperity thousands of years later, see ourselves as if we went out of Egypt? What can we do to experience, in some small way, what our ancestors went through, and make that experience part of us?

Goals: Students will:

1. Identify different ways in which we remember the Exodus story on Passover.
2. Explore what it means to see ourselves as if we went out of Egypt.
3. Reflect on how putting ourselves in the shoes of the Israelite slaves can make us more sensitive to others who are in distress.

Introduction

The central mitzvah of Passover is to remember the Exodus from Egypt: "...Remember this day, on which you came out of Egypt, from the place where you were enslaved, for Adonai brought you out of there with a mighty hand...." (Exodus 13:3) But it is not enough merely to remember. According to the haggadah, we must also see ourselves as if we were freed from Egypt. This task is very difficult. Our lives are so different than those of the slaves in Egypt; how can we possibly put ourselves in their shoes? In this lesson, we talk about the different ways that the Passover seder helps us to make the memory of slavery in Egypt a lived experience that is part of each one of us.

Materials Needed

- Vegetables, such as parsley, celery, or potatoes, and salt water
- A jar of horseradish
- Matzah
- *Charoset* (for an easy, kid-friendly recipe, see www.behrmanhouse.com/holidays-values)

(Bring enough of each of these foods to give each student a sample. And be sure to check first with the education director about synagogue rules regarding keeping kosher and allergies.)

Activities

1. Getting Started: A Slave in Egypt (10 minutes)

Ask students to respond to the journal prompts on page 68. Then ask a few students to volunteer to read their responses to the class. As they read, make sure to review the main events of the Passover story. (See www.behrmanhouse.com/holidays-values for a link to a good retelling of the story.)

Discuss: Why do you think it is important to see ourselves as if we were slaves in Egypt? Allow students to brainstorm a few ideas and then tell them that we will be discussing this question in depth in the next lesson.

2. A Taste of the Exodus (20 minutes)

At the seder, the central mitzvah is to remember the Israelites' Exodus from Egypt. One way of doing so is by eating special foods.

Give every student a taste of the vegetable and salt water, and give them a minute to write down their reactions in the chart on page 69 of the journal. Encourage them to give as much concrete detail as possible. Repeat for each of the foods.

After tasting each food, ask the class: Based on your observations, why do you think we eat this food at the seder and what do you think it represents? Then discuss the traditional explanation of why we eat that food, making sure to cover the following:

- *Karpas* (vegetables and salt water): When the seder was first developed, it was customary to begin a meal with dipped vegetables. The salt water is said to represent the tears the Israelites shed in slavery.
- Matzah: The Torah tells us that matzah is the "bread of affliction," the bread of poor people (most likely what the Israelites ate when they were slaves). Matzah reminds us of the Exodus from Egypt, when the Israelites left so speedily that they didn't have time to wait for their bread dough to rise. (See Deuteronomy 16:3.)
- *Maror* represents the bitterness of slavery.
- *Charoset* represents the mortar the Israelites used when constructing buildings for Pharaoh.

After eating all of the foods, discuss:

- How does eating these foods help you learn about and remember the Exodus from Egypt?
- How was the experience of eating these foods different than just telling the Exodus story with words?
- How does eating these special foods help us to see ourselves as if we went out of Egypt?

Note that the seder is full of strategies to help us make the experience of the Exodus more real and to internalize it. Through eating the different foods, we use all of our senses to experience, in a physical way, some small part of what the Israelites went through.

Review with students the foods that are on the seder plate, including the *karpas*, *maror*, and *charoset*, which they just tasted, as well as the *beitzah* (roasted egg), which symbolizes new life and also reminds us of the Temple sacrifice; the *z'roa* (roasted shank bone), which reminds us of the paschal lamb; and the *chazeret*, the second bitter vegetable (often lettuce is used). You can find more information on these items in a haggadah or in the Further Resources section, below.

3. Four Questions (10 minutes)

Another strategy that the seder uses to help us internalize the Israelites' experience is to encourage participants to ask questions. The seder begins with the Mah Nishtanah. Chant the Four Questions together with your class and read the English translation out loud.

As a class, discuss some possible answers to the four questions. Make sure students understand the meaning of *chameitz*—what kinds of foods are considered *chameitz* and why we don't eat *chameitz* on Passover (see the image on page 71 of the journal). See www.behrmanhouse.com/holidays-values for more about the Four Questions and a discussion of *chameitz*.

Although the four questions of the Mah Nishtanah are fixed, we are also encouraged to ask our own questions. Now that the students have been reminded of some of the central elements of the seder and the Exodus story, ask students to write their own Four Questions on page 71 of their journals. Be sure to make time either in this lesson or in the lessons that follow to address those questions.

4. Wrapping It Up: Values in Action: In Every Generation (10 minutes)

Explain that in every generation, Jews strive to see themselves as if they went out of Egypt. One way to understand this idea is to see the redemption—the act of being freed—from Egypt not just as a one-time event, but as a theme that repeats itself throughout Jewish history. In each generation, we are redeemed from Egypt (the Hebrew name for Egypt, *Mitzrayim*, comes from the root *tzar*, a narrow, constricting place), though the names and details are different each time.

Ask students to choose one of the events from Jewish history on pages 72-73 of the journal and imagine that they were there. Let volunteers act out their imagined experiences in small groups. For further resources on each of these events, see www.behrmanhouse.com/holidays-values.

Enrichment Options

The Seder Plate: As part of Activity 2, "A Taste of the Exodus," bring in a seder plate and identify the different symbols on the plate. Students may also make their own seder plates. In the space for each food, students can write about or illustrate the meaning behind that food (e.g., the bitterness of slavery for *maror*).

The Four Children: After the Mah Nishtanah, the haggadah tells us of the four children who each ask their own questions about Passover. Just as the four children ask different questions based on their unique personalities, backgrounds, and skills, so, too, we each ask different questions. In pairs, students compare the questions they wrote in the "Four Questions" activity and discuss:

- Were your questions similar to or different from other students' questions? How so?
- At the seder, we talk about four different children, who each ask different kinds of questions. Why do you think it is important at the seder to make space for different children to ask different questions?

My Redemption from Egypt: Explain that not only are we redeemed as a people from Egypt in every generation, but each one of us here today is redeemed individually in some small way. Each of us knows what it means to have something that makes us sad or scared or angry, something that prevents us from being the person we want to be. Invite students to share with the class or write about a time that they were able to overcome obstacles that had held them back, whether kids in their school were being mean, whether they were scared to speak in front of a large audience, or whether they really wanted to become friends with the new girl down the block but were afraid to knock on her door.

Further Resources

For more information on the symbolism of the foods on the seder plate, see www.behrmanhouse.com/holidays-values.

Lesson 18: *Ahavat Hager:* Loving the Stranger

Essential Question: How does seeing ourselves as if we went out of Egypt guide our actions?

Goals: Students will:

1. Explore what it means to act as if we went out of Egypt.
2. Understand the mitzvah of *ahavat hager*, loving the stranger as yourself.
3. Reflect on how we can develop empathy for the strangers in our schools and our communities and act on it.

Introduction

In the last lesson, we explored the different strategies we use at the seder to help us see ourselves as though we had been freed from Egypt. Now we ask the bigger question: Why is it important to see ourselves that way? Ideally, seeing ourselves as if we had gone out of Egypt guides our actions. If I know what it is like to be a slave—to be oppressed, to be persecuted, to be different, to be unable to control my own destiny—I will act to help others in similar situations. I will demonstrate understanding and empathy for the suffering of others.

Over and over again (36 times), the Torah tells us to love the stranger because we were once strangers in Egypt. In this lesson, we will explore what it means to love the stranger as ourselves and how we can fulfill this mitzvah today. We will discuss how putting ourselves in someone else's shoes—especially someone who is needy and alone—can help us figure out how to help that person.

Activities

1. Getting Started: "Avadim Hayinu" (5 minutes)

Sing "Avadim Hayinu" together and read the translation in the journal, page 74, out loud. Ask: Why does this song say that "*we* were slaves and now *we* are freed"? Why doesn't it use the word *they*?

Explain that in the last class, we discussed different ways that we can see ourselves as if we had gone out of Egypt, as the song emphasizes. Now we are going to focus on why this is important.

Discuss: How can seeing ourselves as if we had been liberated from Egypt guide our actions? Use this discussion to talk about what it means to have empathy for someone. (*Seeing ourselves as if we went out of Egypt can help us have empathy for people in similar situations; we can understand what they are going through and therefore act with compassion toward them.)*

See www.behrmanhouse.com/holidays-values for a recording of "Avadim Hayinu."

2. Loving the Stranger (15 minutes)

Read the text on page 74 of the journal together out loud. Explain that a stranger in the Torah does not mean someone we don't know, but someone who is an outsider in society, who doesn't belong to the majority group, such as a non-Israelite who lived in the land of Israel when it was under Israelite rule. How would this stranger feel? Why does this person need protection?

Write the word *stranger* inside a circle in the middle of the board. Ask students to fill in the blank: "A stranger is someone who is..." Write their answers around the circle. Do not repeat answers. (*Answers may include: different, needy, vulnerable, alone, taken advantage of, persecuted.*) Encourage students to think as broadly as possible. If students need help jump-starting their thinking, point out that in the Torah, the stranger is often grouped with the orphan and widow. What do these three have in common?

Then split the students into *chevruta* pairs to answer the questions that follow the text. (*"Love the stranger as yourself" means acting to help others who are left out or in need. It might include donating gently used clothes to a shelter, visiting someone who is sick, being friendly to the new kid in class, baking a cake for the new family on the block, or speaking out to make public institutions handicapped-accessible.*)

3. What Would You Do? (15 minutes)

Students read the scenario on page 75 of the journal independently and fill in their responses. If there's time, students can act out the scenario and different possible outcomes.

Bring the class together to discuss:

- How did you write about the situation differently from your eyes and from Becky's eyes?
- Did it change the way you thought about the situation when you saw it from Becky's perspective? How so?
- In *To Kill a Mockingbird,* novelist Harper Lee writes, "You never really know a man until you stand in his shoes and walk around in them." What does this quote teach us? Do you agree? Why or why not?
- Read together the quote from Sforno (a sixteenth-century Italian Jewish philosopher and Bible commentator) and discuss what he would have said we should do in this situation.

4. Wrapping It Up: Making Meaning: *Ahavat Hager* (10 minutes)

Introduce the value *ahavat hager* and its definition, "loving the stranger." Explain that the situation on page 75 is an example of one in which we can demonstrate *ahavat hager* in our own schools and communities. Challenge students to think of other examples.

Ask students to use words or images to describe someone in their own life who could be considered a stranger. How does that person feel? Ask students to illustrate one idea they have for helping that person. If there is time, students can share what they drew with a partner.

Further Resources

Visit www.behrmanhouse.com/holidays-values for a discussion of what it means to act as if we went out of Egypt.

Lesson 19: Strangers in Our World

Essential Question: How can we help the strangers in our world today?

Goals: Students will:

1. Explore ways of loving the stranger in our world today.
2. Choose and develop a class project that aims to help the stranger.

Introduction

Whereas the second lesson focused on what it means to love the stranger as yourself within our schools and our communities, the third lesson brings the mitzvah of loving the stranger as yourself to a more global level, focusing on social justice work that helps the vulnerable throughout the world (Jews and non-Jews). Students will think strategically about what they can do to make a difference. They will continue to explore what it means to develop empathy for someone—even if that someone lives across the globe and does not share our way of life. The lesson will culminate in a social justice project to help the stranger on a global level.

Materials Needed

- Box of matzah
- If possible, computers with Internet access to research various social justice organizations and opportunities. Alternatively, the teacher can hand out information from the Internet about relevant organizations. (See Activity 2 below.) See www.behrmanhouse.com/holidays-values for links to organizations that work to help the stranger.

Activities

1. Getting Started: Matzah, the Bread of Affliction (5 minutes)

Give one student a piece of matzah to hold up. He or she should recite the declaration from the haggadah, on page 77 of the journal, "This is the bread of affliction…."

Then distribute matzah for all the students to taste while answering the questions that follow as a class. Matzah is described in Deuteronomy 16:3 as *lechem oni,* "bread of affliction" or "poor man's bread." Eating matzah reminds us of what it was like to be a slave in Egypt, when we did not have time for our bread to rise. When we eat matzah, we develop empathy for all of those in our community who are poor, needy, or alone—the strangers in our community.

2. Values in Action: Loving the Stranger (20 minutes)

Explain to the students that soon the class will develop its own project to help the stranger. In order to start us thinking about different directions this project can take, we are going to look more closely at five different ways to help the stranger in our world.

Today, loving the stranger is often not as direct and straightforward as inviting the poor and lonely people in our community to eat with us (although it can be). Television and Internet have expanded our world, bringing images of strangers into our homes from across the globe. We are challenged to develop empathy not only for the strangers in our own communities, but for strangers in need throughout the world. Helping these strangers may take a very different form than simply inviting them into our homes; it may require national or international relief organizations, numerous volunteers and staff who are the intermediaries between us and the stranger, and, of course, money. What are some of the opportunities in our world today to help the stranger? And how do we choose between the hundreds of opportunities available?

Divide the students into four small groups, each of which is assigned one of the images in the journal, page 78. Each group should provide some details about what is happening in the image and then make an argument for why this particular way of helping the stranger is important. If possible, each group should do some research on the Internet about organizations or people that help the stranger in this way and how they go about doing it. The teacher may also hand out printouts from the Internet to help each group better understand its topic.

Then each group presents its findings and argument to the class.

3. What Can We Do to Help? (20 minutes)

Based on their work above, encourage students to brainstorm a list of possible class projects to help the stranger. The list could include a fundraiser, such as a car wash or a bake sale, to raise money for one of the organizations discussed. The list could also include a volunteer project, such as visiting isolated elderly in their homes or in a nursing home, or serving a meal in a soup kitchen.

Discuss which option would be best for the class. If students need help with this, prompt them to consider: What is the biggest need? Would we prefer to raise money or to volunteer? Would we like to help people close by or far away? Is it important to us to help the Jewish community in particular? What can we do that will have the biggest impact? How can we measure our impact?

Then have students vote on a project and plan the first few specific steps toward their goal, using the planning chart on page 79 of the journal.

4. Wrapping It Up (5 minutes)

Discuss with students: How is this project connected to the Passover seder? Invite students to share something about their project at their family seder.

Enrichment Options

Elijah the Prophet: At the seder, after the festive meal, we pour a fifth glass of wine for Elijah the prophet and open the door to welcome him into our homes. According to tradition, Elijah will bring in a new age of peace and joy in the world, so we open the door to him to represent our hope that this new age will come soon—even today. Write a wish list or prayer listing all the things you would like to see happen in order to make this world more peaceful and joyful. For example, "I pray that all elderly people will be surrounded by friends and loved ones; I wish that every child had as much food to eat as she or he needs; I pray that every child will be able to go to school."

Chapter

9

YOM HASHOAH AND YOM HA'ATZMA'UT

Remembrance • *Zikaron*, and Jewish Community • *K'lal Yisrael*

Yom Hashoah is a modern holiday created in order to remember the Holocaust. On Yom Hashoah, we remember the incredible loss the Jewish people suffered during WWII. In addition, we remember how people stood up to the Nazis—whether by fighting to survive and going on to build Jewish lives after the war, by resisting the Nazis as partisans or during the Warsaw Ghetto and other uprisings, or by taking courageous actions to save lives. The date for Yom Hashoah was chosen because it is the anniversary of the Warsaw Ghetto Uprising.

Yom Ha'atzma'ut celebrates the establishment of the State of Israel in 1948. On this holiday, we remember the hardships and sacrifices our people endured while working to build the land of Israel, and we celebrate modern Israel's independence and accomplishments.

In this chapter, we explore these topics through the lenses of remembrance, *zikaron*, and Jewish community, *k'lal Yisrael.* In lesson 20, we will consider why it is important to remember the past and how our actions today add to our hopes for the future of the Jewish people. In lesson 21, we will look at ways in which the Jewish world community unites to celebrate the history, land, people, and culture of Israel, our homeland.

Lesson 20: Yom Hashoah: Holocaust Remembrance Day

Essential Questions: Why is it important to remember and commemorate the Holocaust? How can remembering the past help us strengthen our future?

Goals: Students will:

1. Learn basic facts about the Holocaust and how Yom Hashoah is observed.
2. Explain the importance of *zikaron*, "remembrance," as a communal responsibility and value.

Introduction

Unlike other holidays that are described in the Torah or were created by the rabbis centuries ago, Yom Hashoah is a modern holiday created to remember the Holocaust. Yom Hashoah provides an opportunity to remember and reflect on one of the darkest periods in our history, and to strengthen Jewish life today in relation to these important events.

Materials Needed

- *Yahrtzeit* candle and matches (get permission from the education director before lighting them)
- Copies or printouts of the Mourner's Kaddish
- Paper
- Markers or colored pencils

Activities

1. Getting Started: Anne Frank (5 minutes)

Ask students to respond privately to the journaling prompt about Anne Frank, at the introduction to the chapter (see journal page 80).

2. Yom Hashoah: Why We Remember the Holocaust (20 minutes)

As a class, watch *Why We Remember the Holocaust*, an 8-minute video from the United States Holocaust Memorial Museum that gives an introduction to the Holocaust. (Visit www.behrmanhouse.com/holidays-values for a link to this video.)

Invite students to write or draw their thoughts, reactions, and questions on page 81 of the journal as they watch the video. You might want to pause halfway through to gauge the mood of the class and answer any questions. Invite students to discuss their reactions afterward.

Ask a student to read aloud the Did You Know on page 82. Discuss which Jewish values that we learned about were demonstrated by those who risked their lives to fight back and help others. (*gevurah, tzedek, ahavat hager*)

3. Lessons from the Torah (5 minutes)

Invite students to read the quote from Deuteronomy 4:9 on page 82 of the journal and, with a *chevruta* partner, to discuss and answer the questions below the passage.

Discuss aloud:

- How is the verse from Deuteronomy relevant to the Holocaust? *(It's about our responsibility to remember something important or terrible.)*
- Why should we remember the Holocaust? (*We honor those who suffered and died by remembering them; we learn from the past in order to avoid mistakes in the future; we are reminded that we all have responsibility toward one another.*)
- How can each of us remember it if we weren't there and if it happened before we were born? (*We can read or listen to the stories of survivors, visit memorials and museums, and talk about the Holocaust in order to keep the memory alive for ourselves and future generations.*)

4. Making Meaning: Zikaron (15 minutes)

The Hebrew word *zikaron* means "remembrance." Ask students to think about an important moment or person from the past whom they remember. Why and how do they remember this person? They can record their thoughts on page 83 of the journal.

Explain that Yizkor is a special service that we recite on Yom Kippur and other holidays in remembrance of loved ones we have lost. The Israeli holiday Yom Hazikaron, or Day of Remembrance, honors those who lost their lives for the State of Israel. The words *Yizkor* and *zikaron* both come from the Hebrew word *zachor*, which means "remember."

Ask students to brainstorm ways we can remember the Holocaust. Give them 5 minutes to work with a partner or in a small group to jot down their ideas in their journals. Then ask them to share with the class. *(Answers might include: light a yahrtzeit candle; say the Mourner's Kaddish, the prayer for those we've lost; watch movies, look at pictures, read poetry; hear a survivor speak or tell their story; observe a moment of silence; read lists of names of the victims; visit museums; read books or stories about the Holocaust; hear stories from family members or friends; ask questions and search for answers.)*

Pass out copies of the Mourner's Kaddish and explain that it is the prayer we say for people we have lost. Light the *yahrtzeit* candle and recite Kaddish with the class for those who died in the Holocaust.

5. Wrapping It Up: Art Connection (10 minutes)

Explain to students that during the Holocaust, many adults and children used art as a way to bring hope and strength to their lives. People played music, wrote stories and poetry, drew and even painted. Ask students to create art to express our responsibility to one another to always remember the Holocaust. It could be a poster, a poem, a drawing, or whatever form of expression they feel most comfortable with. Students can use the space in their journal, page 84, or a separate paper. Let students finish their projects at home if they need more time.

Enrichment Options

Art Connection On Display: Let students take their artwork to the next level. Encourage them to edit, revise, and otherwise fine-tune their projects, and to sign them. Frame or mount the art on sturdy backing, and create a display case or bulletin board of your students' artistic expressions. Invite other classes to view it. As an alternative, photograph each piece and create a digital booklet to be shared with families.

Further Resources

Visit www.behrmanhouse.com/holidays-values for links to resources and supplements for educators on the websites of Yad Vashem and the United States Holocaust Memorial Museum, as well as a fascinating story about the Paper Clips project, an effort by children in Tennessee to understand the magnitude of human loss during the Holocaust.

Lesson 21: Yom Ha'atzma'ut: Israel's Independence Day

Essential Questions: How is Israel unique? How do our celebrations for Yom Ha'atzma'ut demonstrate the value of *k'lal Yisrael,* the unity of the world Jewish community?

Goals: Students will:

1. Explain the concept of *k'lal Yisrael*, the idea that Jews all over the world share history, culture, and values, and that Yom Ha'atzma'ut is a time to celebrate our unity and our homeland.
2. Recognize that Jews fought to build a homeland, a place where we would be safe and free to be Jewish.
3. Learn about the culture and special features of Israel that make it unique and important to us.

Introduction

On Yom Ha'atzma'ut, we reflect on the hardships and sacrifices people endured while working to build the modern State of Israel. We recognize that people from all over the world worked to create a Jewish homeland, driven by the concept of *k'lal Yisrael.* Together with Jews everywhere, we celebrate Israel and its accomplishments, history, and culture.

Materials

- Traditional Israeli foods: tomato and cucumber salad, pita and hummus, dates, oranges. Or, try making a traditional Israeli breakfast. See Further Resources for the link.
- Israeli folk music or modern Hebrew music (see suggestions in resource list)
- Travel photos of Israel (see "Advance Preparation")

Advance Preparation

Ask students and other teachers who have been to Israel to bring in photos from their trips. You can also print photos of Israel from online and bring those in.

Activities

1. Getting Started: A Modern Jewish State (5 minutes)

Ask students to respond privately to the journaling prompt about Theodor Herzl (see student book page 85). Check for understanding of the quote, first.

2. Yom Ha'atzma'ut: Israel's Independence Day (10 minutes)

Ask students what they think Independence Day is about, and what are typical ways of celebrating. (*It's about becoming free from being ruled by others; creating your own government/laws; celebrating freedom—of religion, speech, thought, expression; having a sense of pride in your land, people, culture, history; it's celebrated with parties, fireworks.*)

Explain that just as we celebrate Independence Day in the United States and Canada Day in Canada, we celebrate the creation of the modern State of Israel on Yom Ha'atzma'ut.

Write the words "Eretz Yisrael", "Medinat Yisrael", and "Am Yisrael" on the board, and ask students if they know the meanings of these phrases. Ask students, in pairs or small groups, to use the key words on page 86 to come up with definitions for these terms. Here are explanations of the terms:

- *Eretz Yisrael* is the Land of Israel. It refers to the land itself, which is described in the Torah, and has been a source of Jewish identity and yearning for thousands of years.
- *Medinat Yisrael* refers to the modern State of Israel, which declared independence in 1948.
- *Am Yisrael* is the people of Israel, meaning the Jewish people, no matter where they live.

Ask if any students have been to Israel. If so, invite them to share memories and photos.

3. Making Meaning: K'lal Yisrael (5 minutes)

Explain that *k'lal Yisrael* means that we are one community. Yom Ha'atzma'ut is a time for all Jews to recognize the values and history that unite us as Jews, and to celebrate our spiritual and historical homeland.

Explain that Israel was established by Jewish people from all over the world. The value of *k'lal Yisrael* inspired them to do what they could to ensure a homeland for all Jews.

4. Building a Jewish State (10 minutes)

Ask students to work in pairs and read about some important events in building the Jewish state on page 87 of the journal. Then, using the pictures and captions as clues, they will place the events in order on the timeline.

The answers, in order, are:

- **First Aliyah, 1882:** The first wave of Jews moves to the land of Israel (then called Palestine) to escape growing violence against Jews throughout Europe. (The Second Aliyah begins in 1904.)
- **Early Zionism, 1897:** Theodor Herzl promotes Zionism, the idea of founding a Jewish state in the land of Israel. He convenes the First Zionist Congress in Switzerland.
- **Kibbutzim, 1909:** The first kibbutz (plural, *kibbutzim*) is founded in Palestine. A kibbutz is a community in which property and responsibilities are shared by all.
- **Modern Hebrew, 1922:** Eliezer Ben-Yehuda leads a movement to transform ancient Hebrew into a modern language. Hebrew becomes the official language of the Jews in Palestine, helping Jews from all over the world talk to each other.
- **The Holocaust, 1939-1945:** Millions of European Jews lose their lives at the hands of the Nazis. Afterward the survivors need a place to go, adding urgency to the Zionists' goal of creating a Jewish nation.
- **Independence, 1948:** David Ben-Gurion, the first prime minister of Israel, announces the establishment of the State of Israel, a place that all Jewish people can call home.

Ask students to identify examples of *k'lal Yisrael* in these events. (*coming to Israel with other Jews to start a new life, promoting a Jewish state for the safety and protection of Jews who are persecuted, building working communities in the land of Israel, establishing a common language based on the ancient Jewish language of prayer and study, providing a safe place for survivors of the Holocaust, establishing Israel as a Jewish state that would always welcome Jews)*

5. Celebrate Israel! (15 minutes)

Explain to students that on Yom Ha'atzma'ut, Israelis love to have fun. Because Yom Ha'atzma'ut begins at the end of Yom Hazikaron, the day that fallen soldiers and victims of terror are remembered, there is a real change in mood! Ask students to read on page 88 of the journal about how Israelis celebrate. Then ask students how they would like to show *k'lal Yisrael* in their celebration of Yom Ha'atzma'ut.

Pass out the Israeli snacks and play some Hebrew music. Visit www.goisrael.com and take a tour of Israel in pictures. Learn an Israeli song or watch a video about Israel (see the Further Resources for this lesson).

6. Wrapping It Up: Did You Know? (5 minutes)

K'lal Yisrael, being a part of the worldwide Jewish community, doesn't mean we're all the same. Even within Israel, there is a lot of diversity within the Jewish community. Ask students to read the Did You Know on page 89 of the journal. What do Jews in each of these groups have in common with each other and with us, as Jews in North America today, and in what ways are we all different?

Ask students how the value of *k'lal Yisrael* is related to *zikaron*, "remembrance." (*Both of these values strengthen our connections with others, build community, show we care.*)

Enrichment Options

The Israeli Flag: Have students research the history and development of the Israeli flag. Learn about its symbolism, who designed it, and when. Have students create their own Israeli flags, incorporating things they learned about Israel in this lesson.

Israeli Songs: Together with the students, learn some of the following songs, and find English translations for the lyrics. Ask students how these songs demonstrate the value of *k'lal Yisrael.*

- "Yerushalayim shel Zahav"
- "Eretz Yisrael Sheli"
- "Rak B'Yisrael"

Further Resources

Visit www.behrmanhouse.com/holidays-values for links to modern Israeli music, classic Israeli dances and songs, and more information about Yom Ha'atzma'ut celebrations in Israel.

Chapter

10

SHAVUOT

Learning from the Torah • *Talmud Torah*

Shavuot celebrates both the giving of the Torah and the beginning of the harvest season, the first fruits. As we complete this book, we look back at the Jewish values we have learned and see how all of these values come from the Torah. Even the Torah's account of how the ancient Israelites harvested the first fruits, which seems so far away from our modern lives, teaches important values such as giving to the poor.

In this concluding lesson, we explore how Talmud Torah, the mitzvah of learning the Torah, can help us in deciding what to do and how to behave in our everyday lives.

Lesson 22: Bringing Jewish Values into Our Lives

Essential Question: How can the Torah help us make choices about what to do and how to behave in our everyday lives?

Goals: Students will:

1. Discuss the customs and history of the holiday of Shavuot.
2. Understand how Jewish values come from the Torah.
3. Reflect on how values from the Torah can shape their lives.

Introduction

In this lesson, we learn the history and experience the rituals of Shavuot, with an eye to how this holiday helps us to celebrate the role of Torah in our lives. We explore how our Jewish values come from the Torah, and how Torah can guide our lives.

Materials Needed

- A few copies of the *Tanach* (the Bible)
- Cheesecake, blintzes, or another dairy treat for the class to share
- Napkins, paper plates
- Optional: recipe and ingredients for making a dairy treat (optional)

Activities

1. Getting Started: The Gift of Torah (5 minutes)

Read the chapter introduction together on page 90 of the journal, then ask students to work in pairs responding to the prompts about the gift of Torah.

2. My Ten Commandments (10 minutes)

Ask the class: What are some of the Ten Commandments? (*Don't steal, honor your parents, keep Shabbat, etc.)* Show students how to look up the Ten Commandments in the *Tanach*, from Exodus chapter 20, and review them as a class.

Explain that the Ten Commandments are considered the most important principles in Judaism. Ask the students to turn to page 91 in their journal and write their own Ten Commandments, the most important principles in their own lives (*such as "Listen to your parents," "Be nice to your siblings," "Work hard at school"*). If there is time, ask students, as a class, to come up with a class list of ten commandments based on their individual lists. Remind the class to debate and listen with *kavod*, respect.

3. Giving from Our Harvest (10 minutes)

One Jewish value that we learn from the Torah is giving to those in need. Ancient Israelite farmers left the corners of their fields and any produce that fell during the harvest process (the gleanings) for poor people to come take. In the book of Ruth, which we read on Shavuot, Boaz leaves the gleanings in his field, and Ruth comes to take them so that she and her mother-in-law, Naomi, will have food.

Ask students to answer the questions on page 92. If there's time, encourage students to think of things they can do as a class to give to the poor in honor of Shavuot (*such as choosing a recipient for the class tzedakah box, donating gently used clothes and books or toys, volunteering at a local soup kitchen*).

4. Dairy on Shavuot (5 minutes)

Read the explanation on page 93 of the journal about the tradition of eating dairy foods on Shavuot. Give students dairy treats, such as a piece of cheesecake. As they are eating, ask: Why do you think the Torah is compared to milk and honey? How is the Torah healthy and sweet?

If you have time and access to a kitchen, your class can make dairy treats together, such as blintzes, to celebrate the sweetness of Torah.

5. Making Meaning: Talmud Torah (5 minutes)

Explain that the study of Torah is itself a mitzvah, a commandment from the Torah. From the Torah we learn important lessons that can help us in deciding what to do and how to behave in our everyday lives.
Ask students to read about Talmud Torah and respond to the prompts on page 93 of the journal privately. Those students who wish to may share their answers with the class.

6. Wrapping It Up: Torah Values (15 minutes)

Ask students to match the Torah verses on page 94 with the Jewish values that they teach. Let students look back through their journals for the answers as needed. Send journals home with students and encourage them to keep the journals and share them with their families.

The answers are:
1. *teshuvah* (return or repentance)
2. *ahavat hager* (loving the stranger)
3. *hakarat hatov* (gratitude)
4. *bal tashchit* (caring for the environment)
5. *anavah* (humility)
6. *gevurah* (courage)
7. *Talmud Torah* (learning from the Torah)
8. *simchah* (rejoicing)
9. *bein kodesh l'chol* (holy time and space)
10. *tzedek* (justice)
11. *tzedakah* (giving)
12. *zikaron* (remembrance)
13. *shalom* (peace)
14. *k'lal Yisrael* (Jewish community)

Enrichment Options

Tikun Leil Shavuot: On the night of Shavuot, there is a tradition of staying up late—even all night!—to study Torah. Invite students and their families to your class's own Tikun Leil Shavuot one evening. Divide students into small groups and assign each group one of the values from this book. Each group prepares a game, song, poem, poster, or play, or chooses another creative medium to teach their families about the value. On the night of the Tikun, each group presents to the other students and their families. You may serve cheesecake or another dairy treat at the event.

Book of Ruth: On Shavuot, we read the book of Ruth, which tells the story of how Ruth joined the Jewish people. Read the story of Ruth together as a class. Ask: What did Ruth do that made her worthy of becoming the great-grandmother of King David? How did she practice Jewish values? See www.behrmanhouse.com/holidays-values for links to the text and a summary of the book of Ruth.

Developing an Action Plan

After each holiday, or at the end of the course, ask students to brainstorm: Which new holiday traditions did you experience this year for the first time? Which Jewish values do you want to build into your life? Make a list of their responses on the board or on a poster, and help students develop an action plan to make changes in their lives, and the lives of others, by committing to trying new holiday experiences and acting on their Jewish values in new ways during the coming weeks, months, and years.

Encourage students to fill in their Action Plan in the journal, page 96, including both holiday experiences and ways they can act on their values.

Project Based Learning

What Is Project Based Learning?

Project Based Learning (PBL) is a teaching strategy that enriches student learning through inquiry. It begins with a driving question—an authentic query about a meaningful topic for students—and ends with learners presenting the results of their work in a public forum, often in a venue other than the classroom. Because PBL gives students a voice in the learning process and promotes real-world experiences, it is well suited to learning about Jewish holidays and values. When properly implemented, project based learning activities will enable students to acquire a deeper understanding of and make personal connections to their Jewish heritage.

Implementing Project Based Learning: Seven Easy Steps

1. The teacher identifies a content area for the project, and goals and objectives to be achieved.
2. The teacher develops a driving question that focuses the project and has authentic meaning for the students.
3. Students generate questions they will need to answer in order to solve the problem.
4. With input from students, the teacher creates a timeline for the project and communicates it to students and parents.
5. Students seek answers to the questions, by interviewing family members, taking field trips, etc. Learning happens at school and/or at home.
6. Teachers and students continually reflect on and evaluate the learning process, while they're working on the project and also when it's completed.
7. Students present their results in a public venue, such as a school assembly, a class art exhibit, a newspaper article, a photo journal, or even a video slideshow. Presentations might include written work, artwork, video, music, and photos.

Using Project Based Learning for *Jewish Holidays, Jewish Values*

The Enrichment Options at the end of many of the lessons in this book include ideas that can be made into project based learning activities, such as a social justice project for Passover, or an environmental project for Tu BiShevat. You can create an authentic, meaningful project based learning experience by following the steps above.

For more information about project based learning, and a helpful graphic organizer template for organizing your project, visit www.behrmanhouse.com/project-based-learning. Also consider using the Online Learning Center, where students can share their progress with group members, blog about issues related to the project, and even present the final project.

Notes